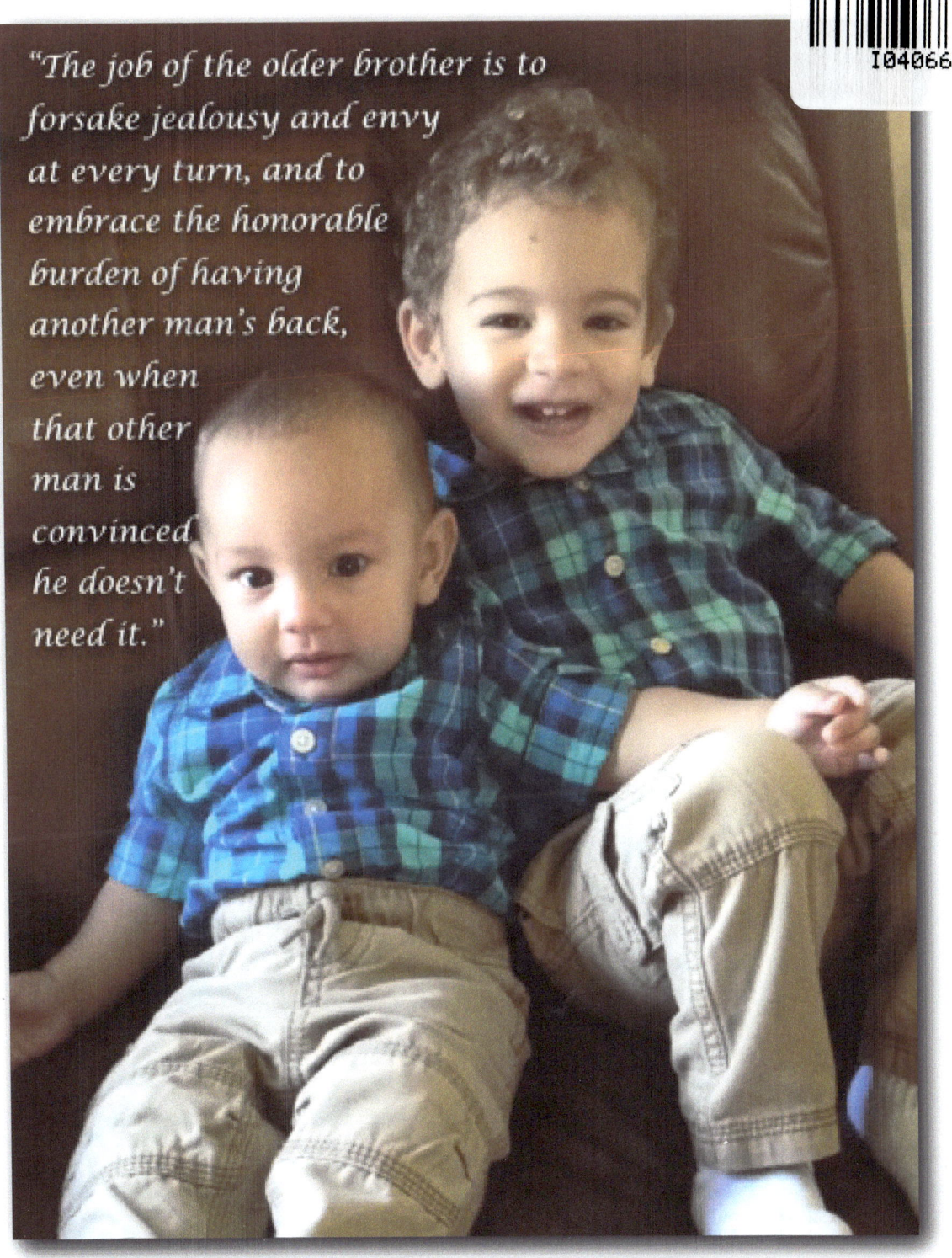

"The job of the older brother is to forsake jealousy and envy at every turn, and to embrace the honorable burden of having another man's back, even when that other man is convinced he doesn't need it."

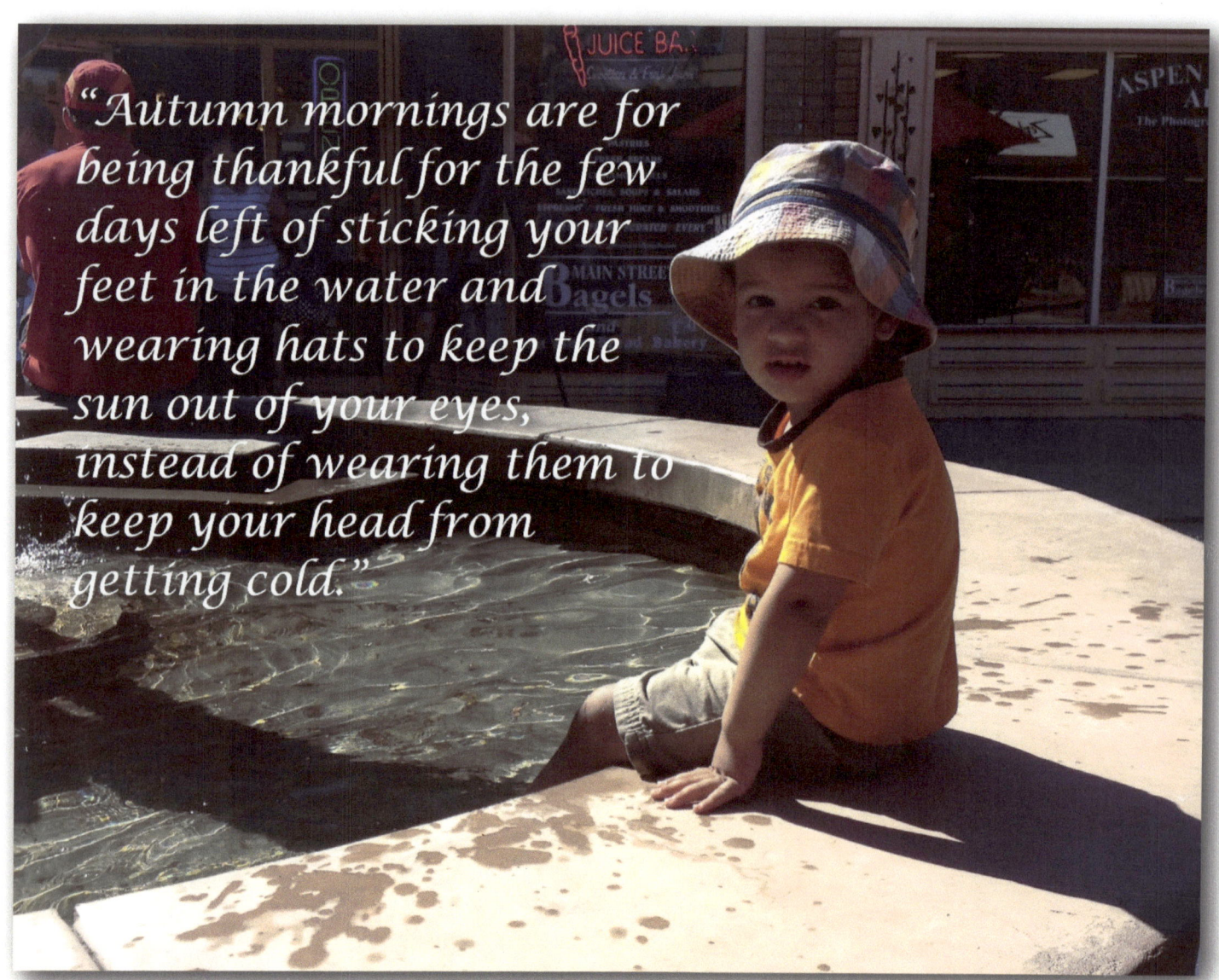

"Autumn mornings are for being thankful for the few days left of sticking your feet in the water and wearing hats to keep the sun out of your eyes, instead of wearing them to keep your head from getting cold."

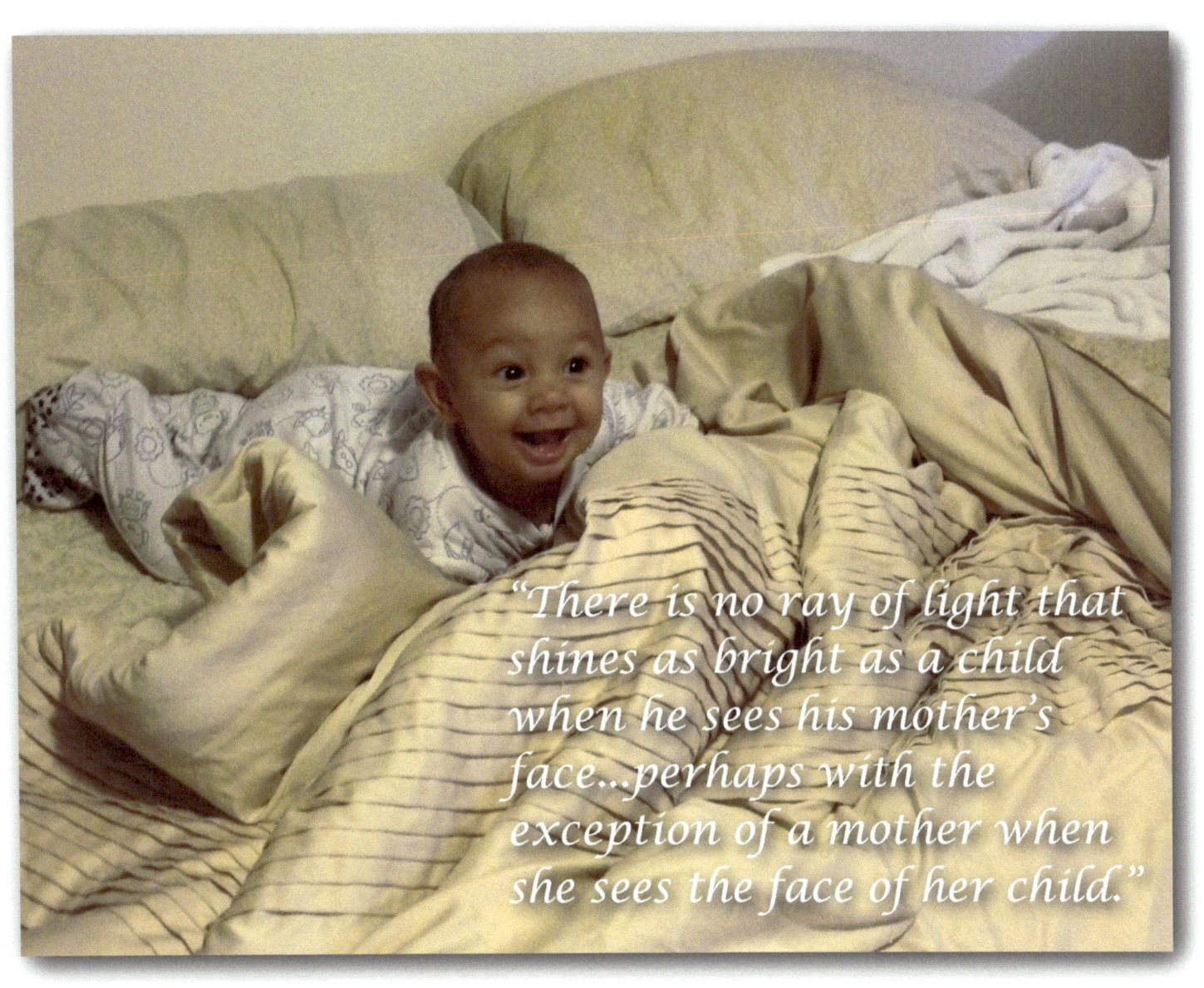

"There is no ray of light that shines as bright as a child when he sees his mother's face...perhaps with the exception of a mother when she sees the face of her child."

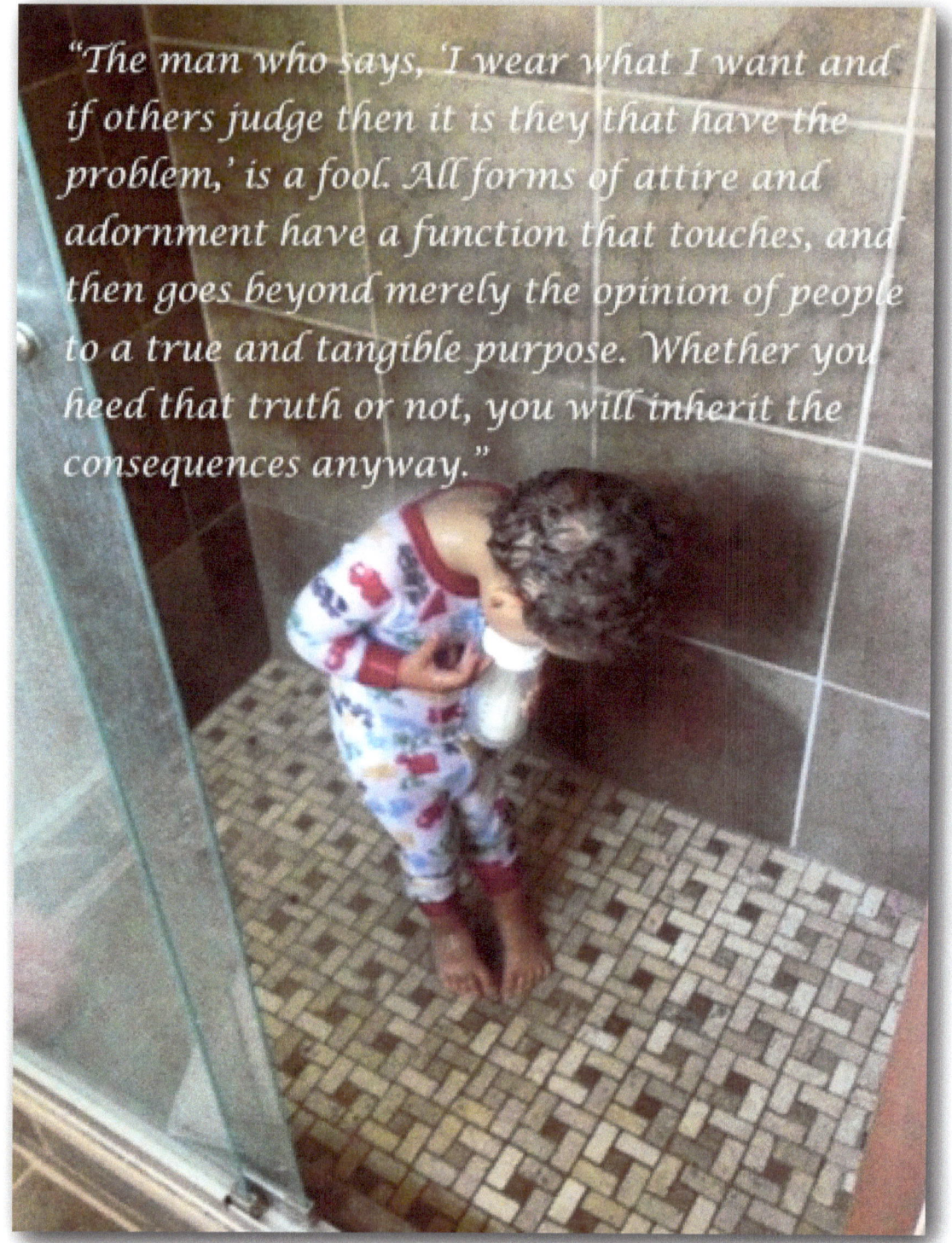

"The man who says, 'I wear what I want and if others judge then it is they that have the problem,' is a fool. All forms of attire and adornment have a function that touches, and then goes beyond merely the opinion of people to a true and tangible purpose. Whether you heed that truth or not, you will inherit the consequences anyway."

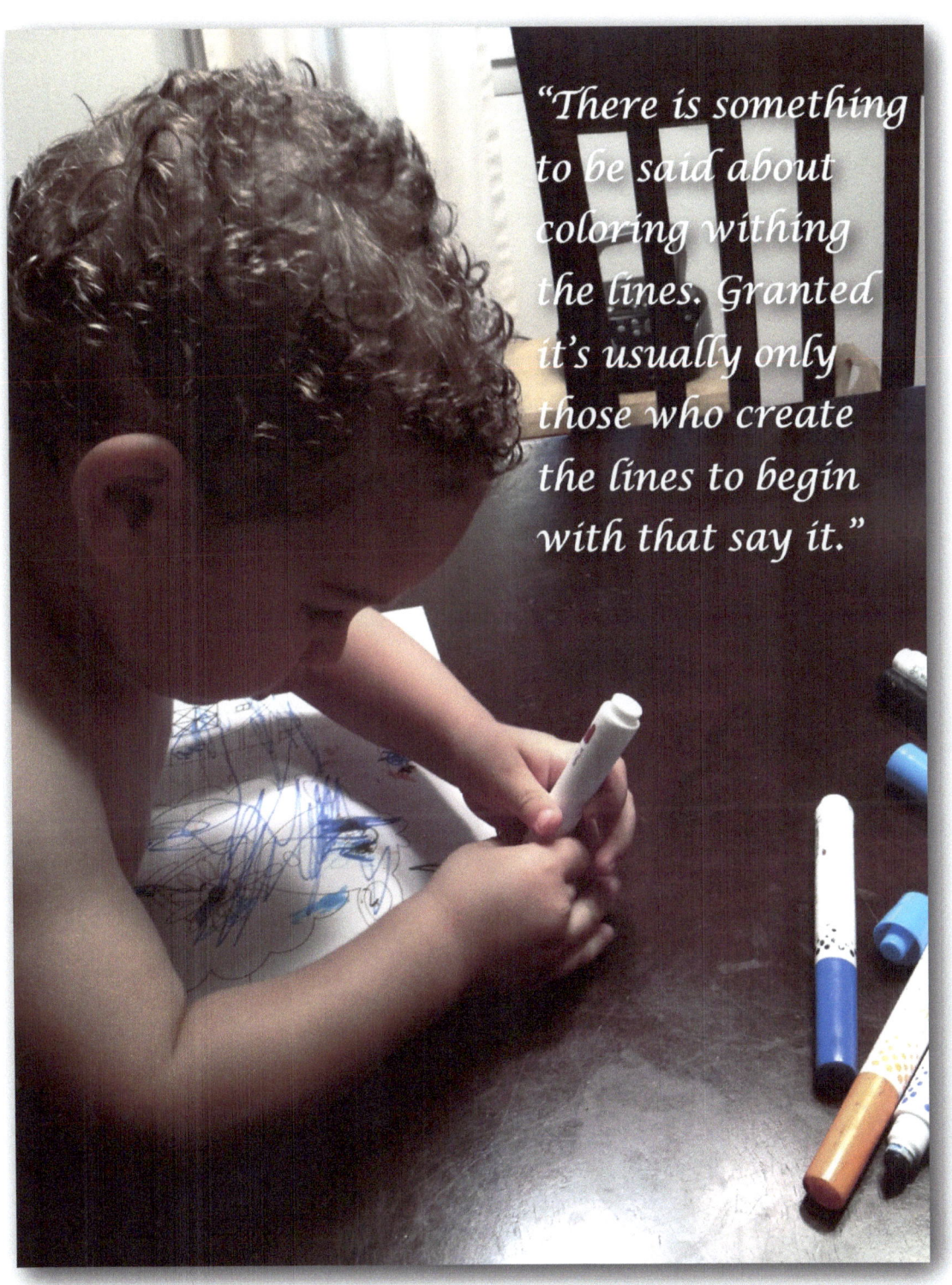

"There is something to be said about coloring withing the lines. Granted it's usually only those who create the lines to begin with that say it."

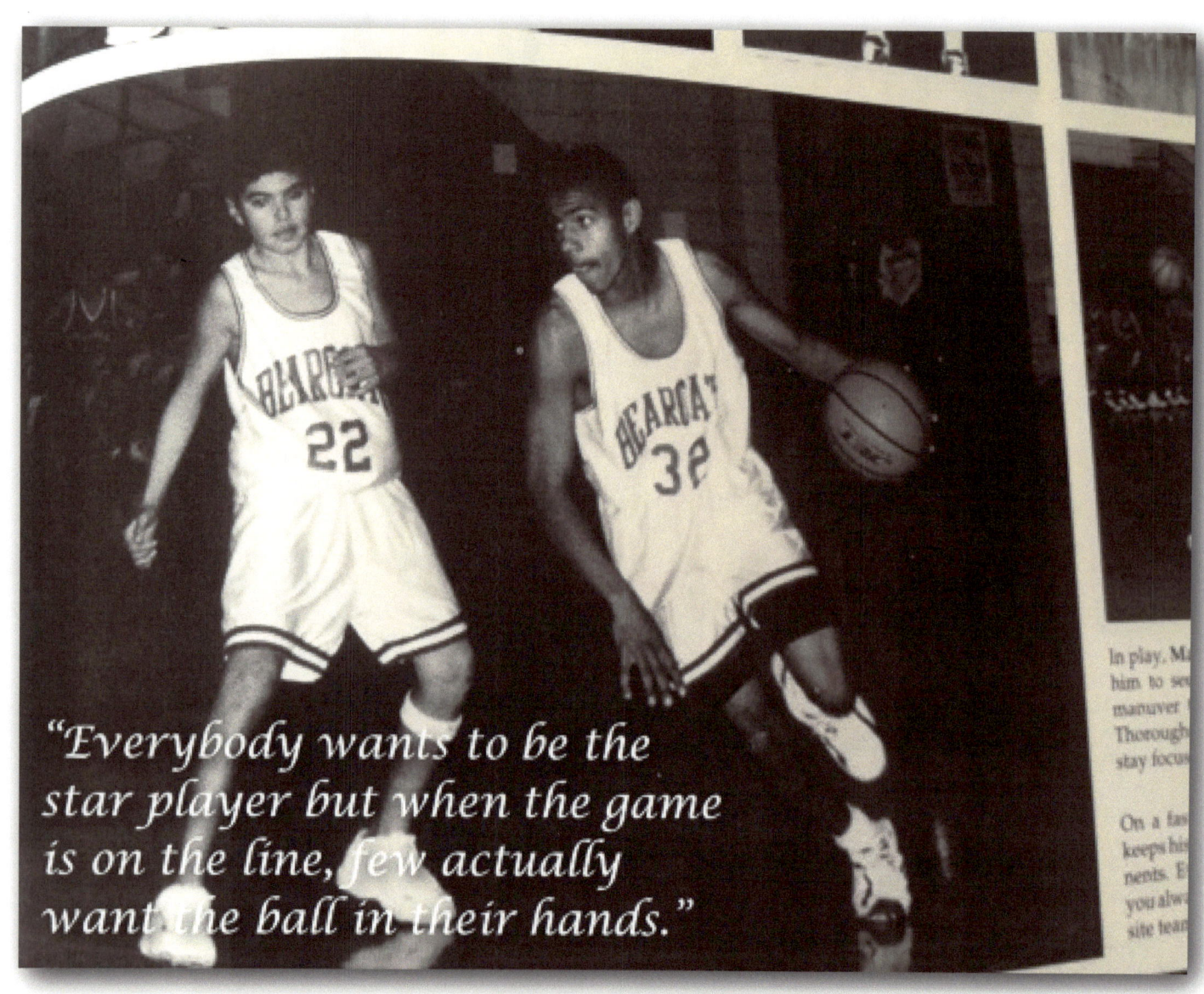

"Everybody wants to be the star player but when the game is on the line, few actually want the ball in their hands."

In play, Ma
him to se
manuver
Thorough
stay focus

On a fas
keeps his
nents. E
you alwa
site team

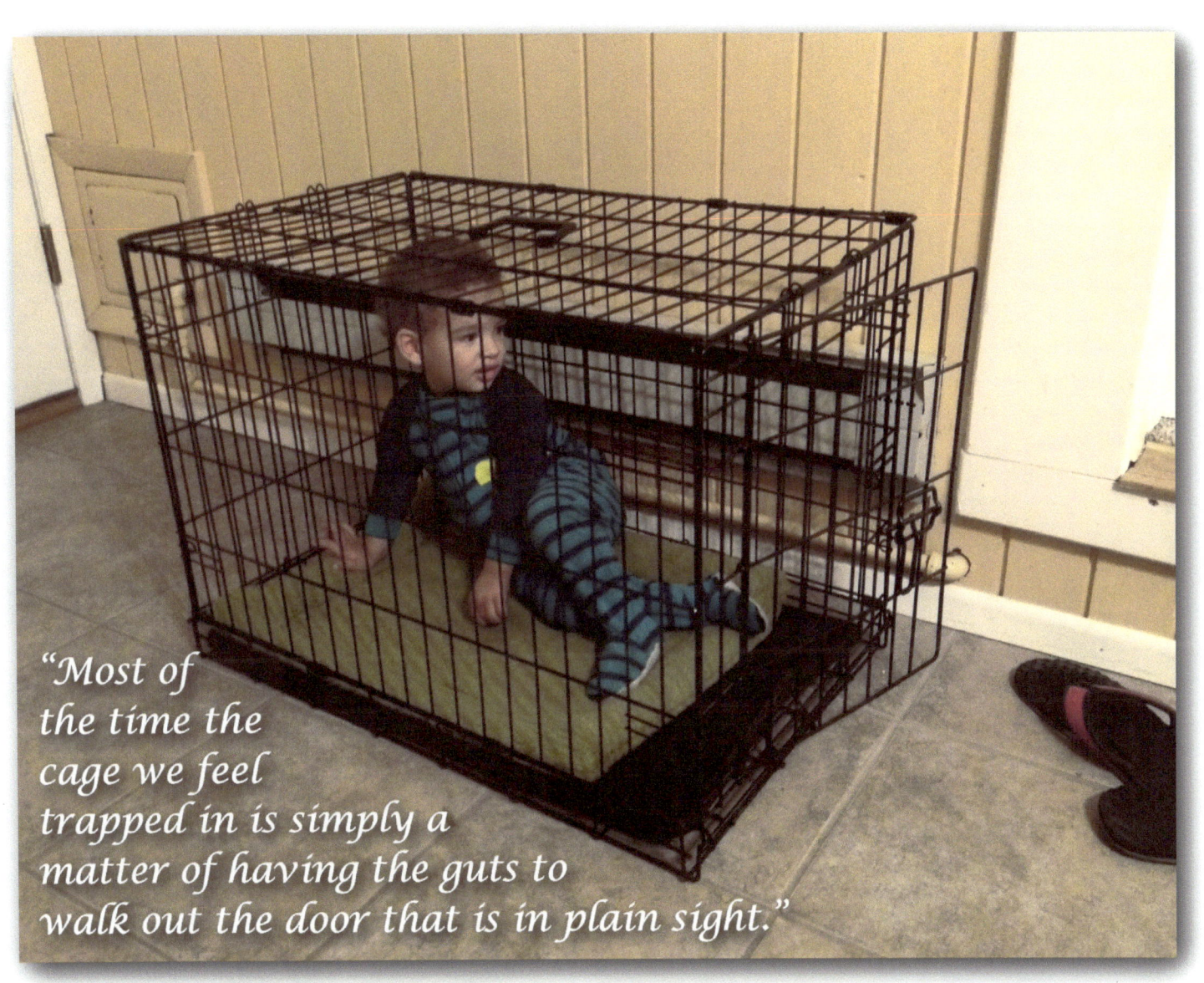

"Most of the time the cage we feel trapped in is simply a matter of having the guts to walk out the door that is in plain sight."

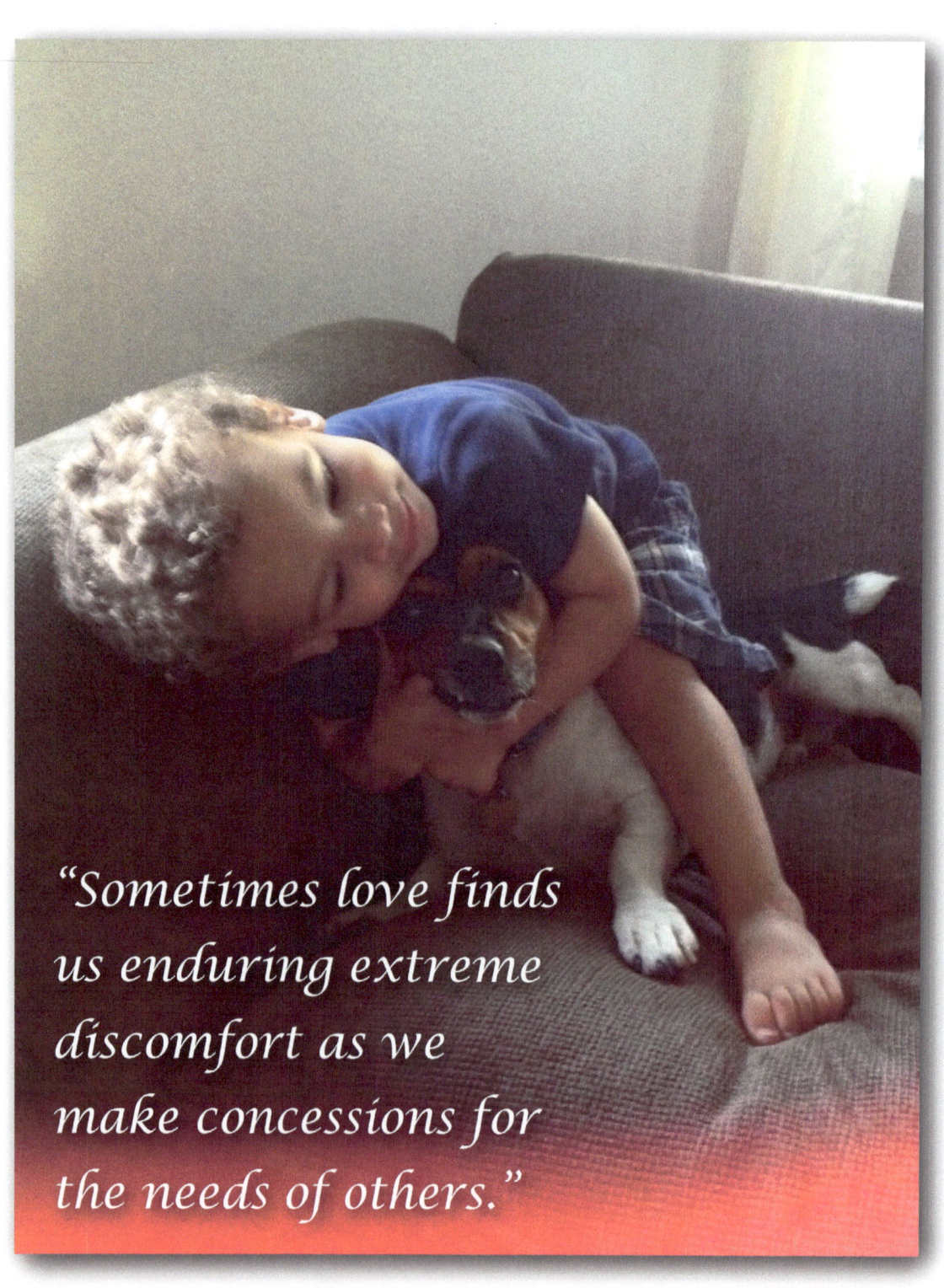

"Sometimes love finds us enduring extreme discomfort as we make concessions for the needs of others."

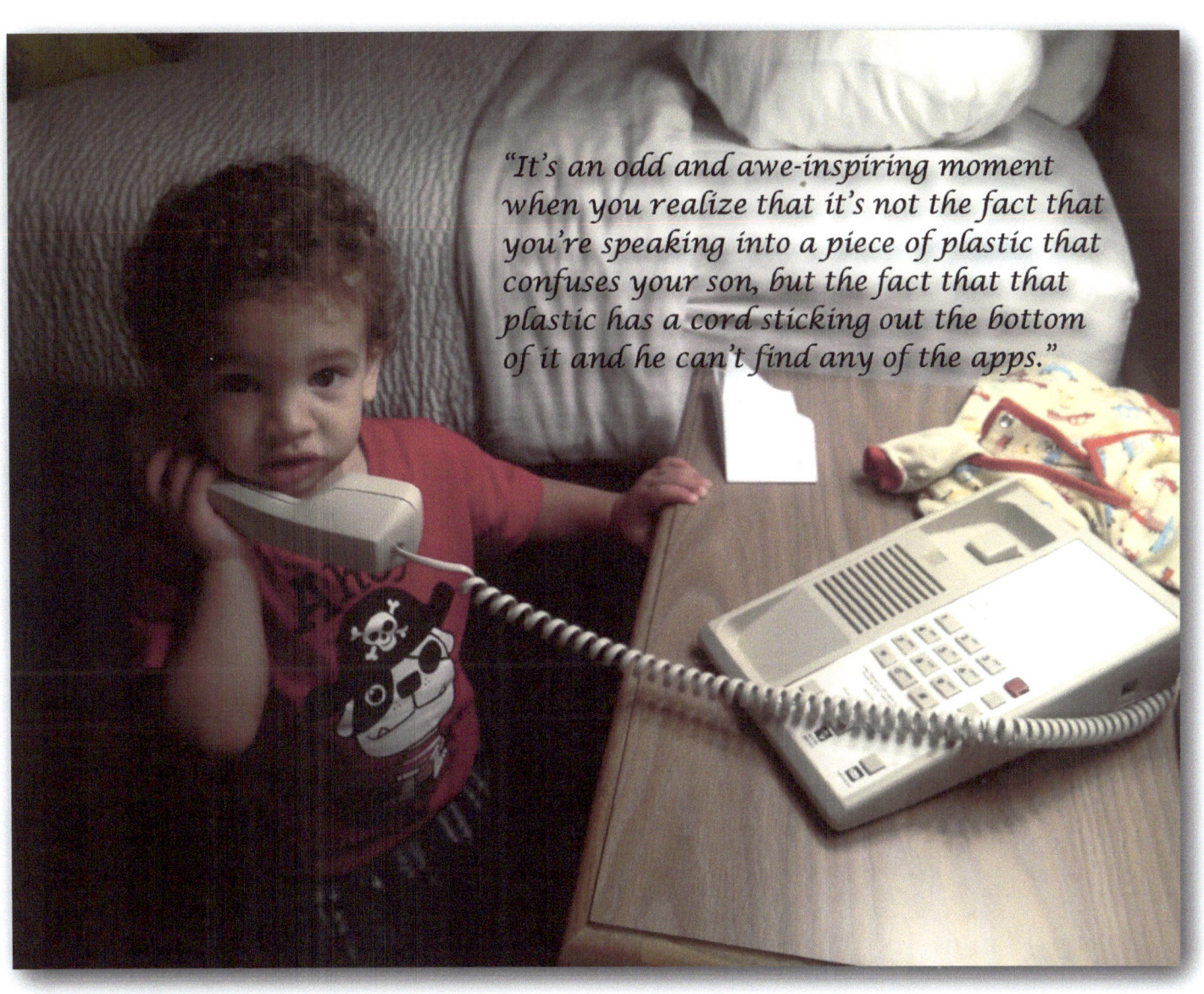

"It's an odd and awe-inspiring moment when you realize that it's not the fact that you're speaking into a piece of plastic that confuses your son, but the fact that that plastic has a cord sticking out the bottom of it and he can't find any of the apps."

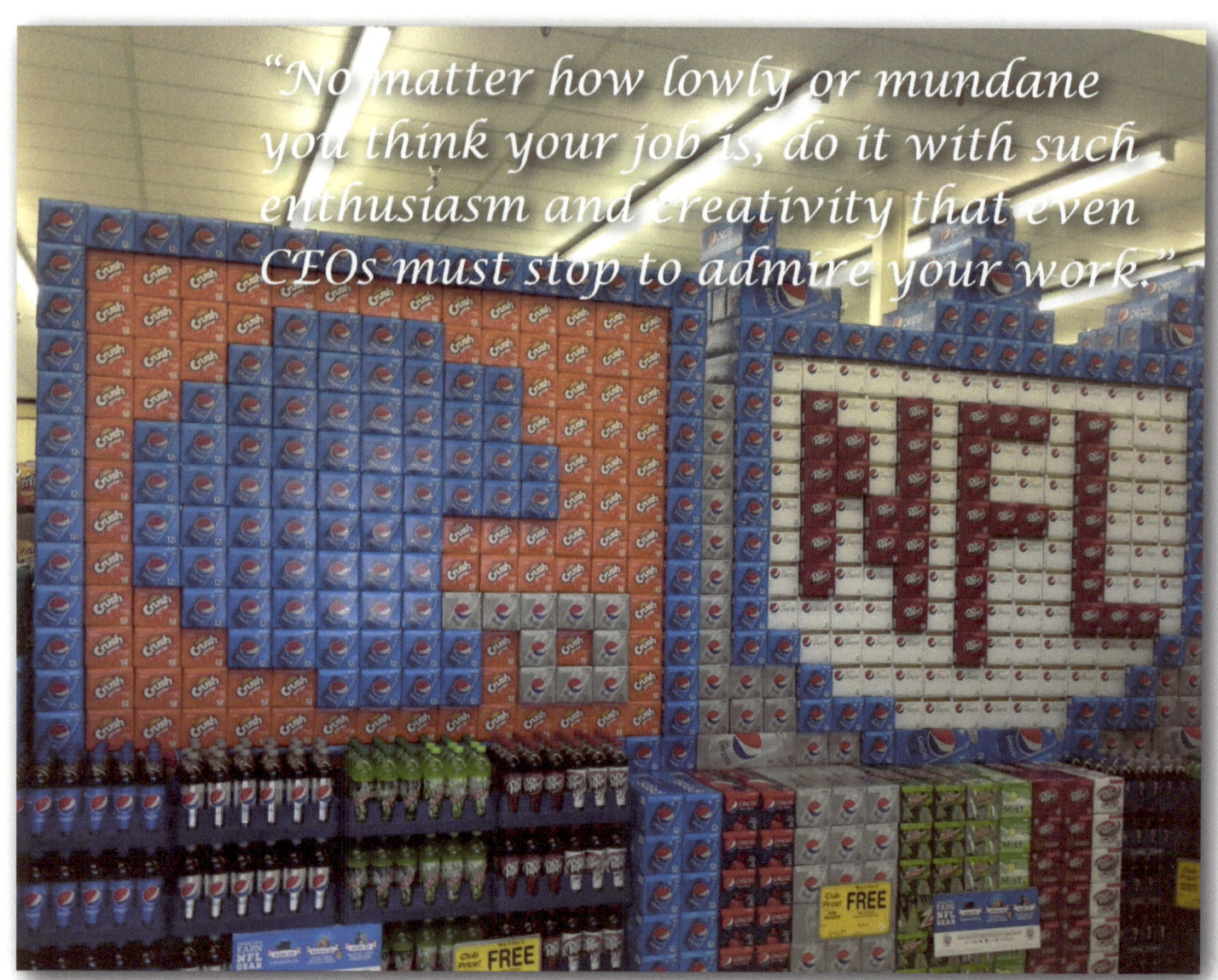

"No matter how lowly or mundane you think your job is, do it with such enthusiasm and creativity that even CEOs must stop to admire your work."

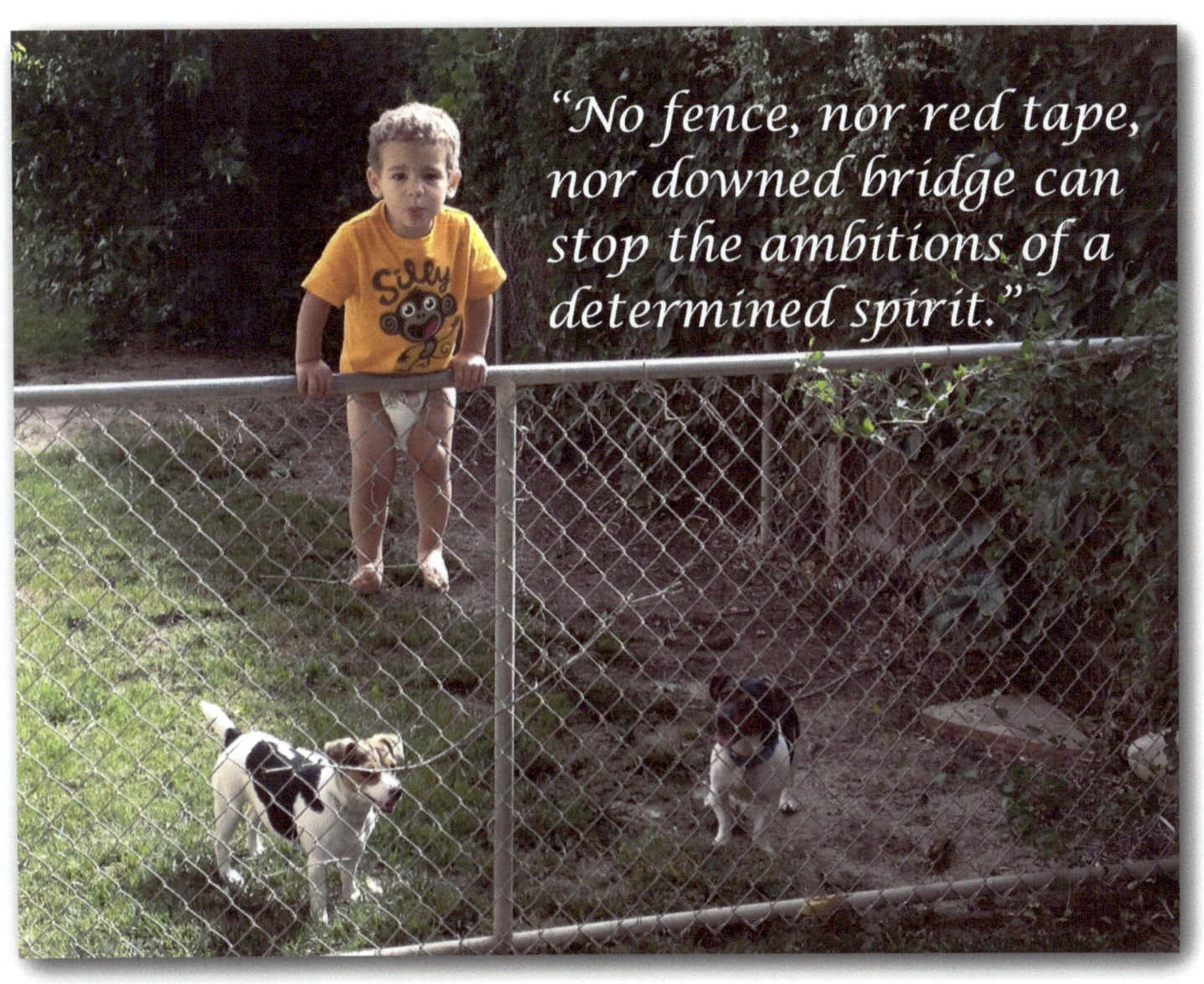

"No fence, nor red tape, nor downed bridge can stop the ambitions of a determined spirit."

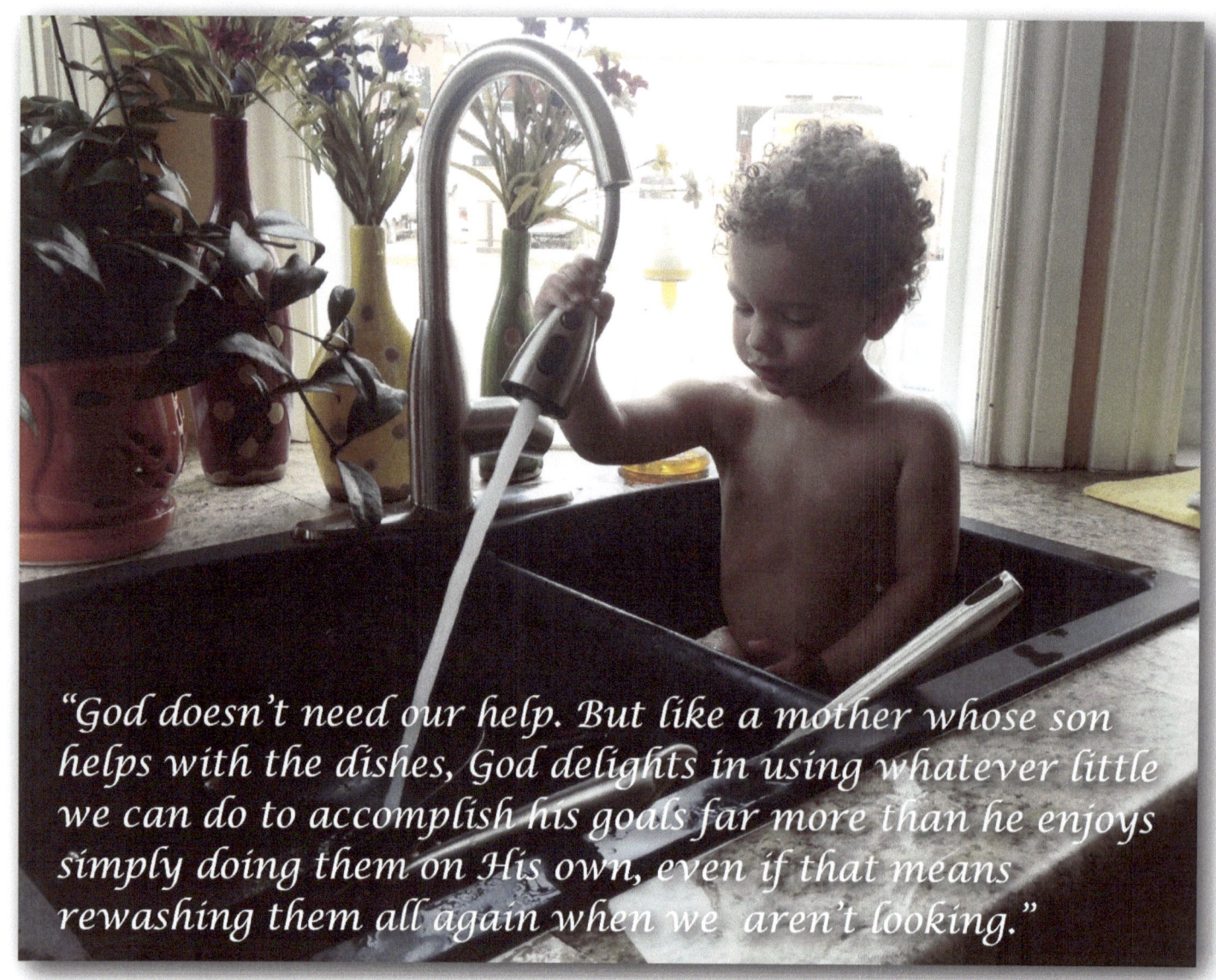

"God doesn't need our help. But like a mother whose son helps with the dishes, God delights in using whatever little we can do to accomplish his goals far more than he enjoys simply doing them on His own, even if that means rewashing them all again when we aren't looking."

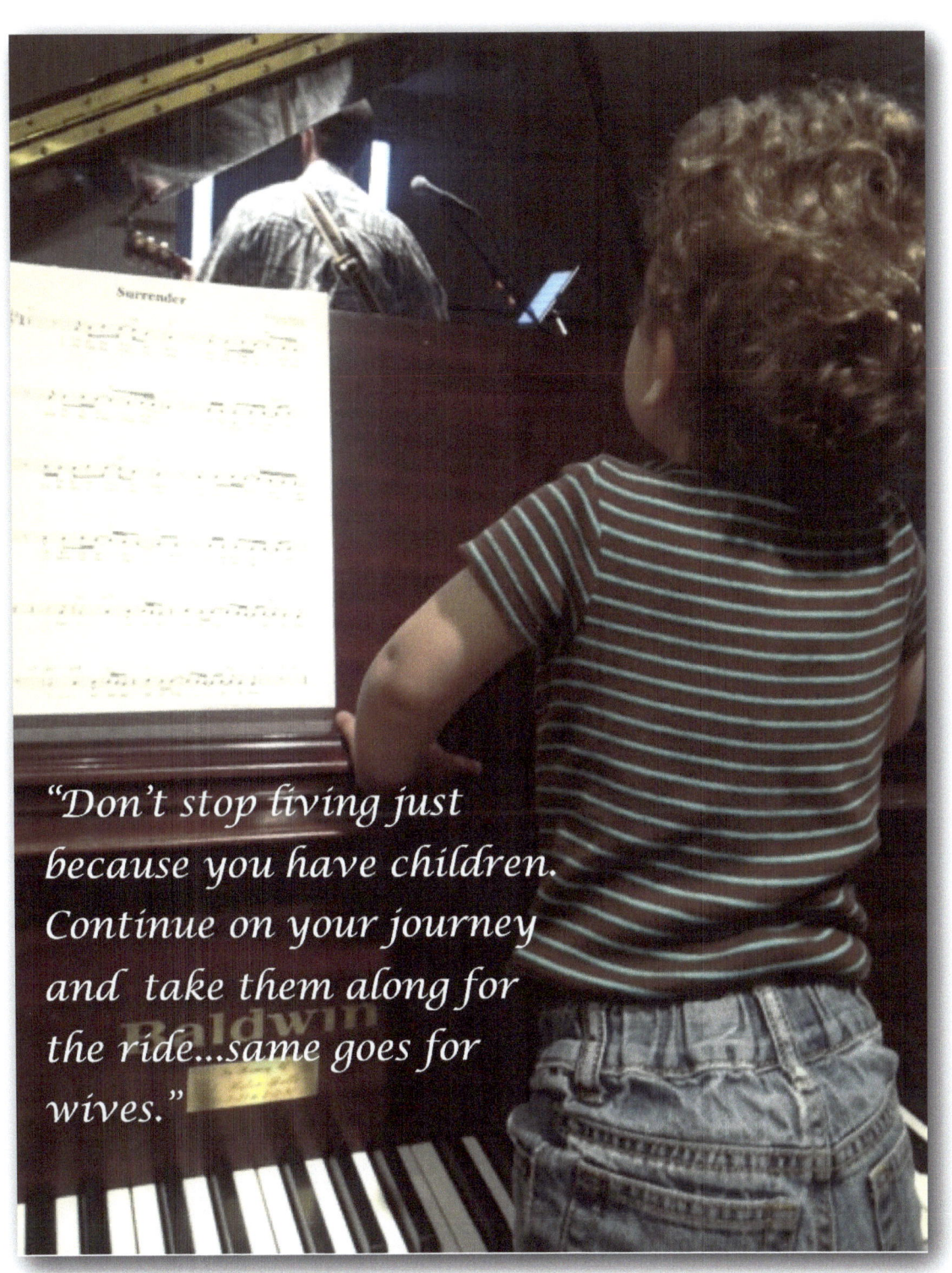

"Don't stop living just because you have children. Continue on your journey and take them along for the ride...same goes for wives."

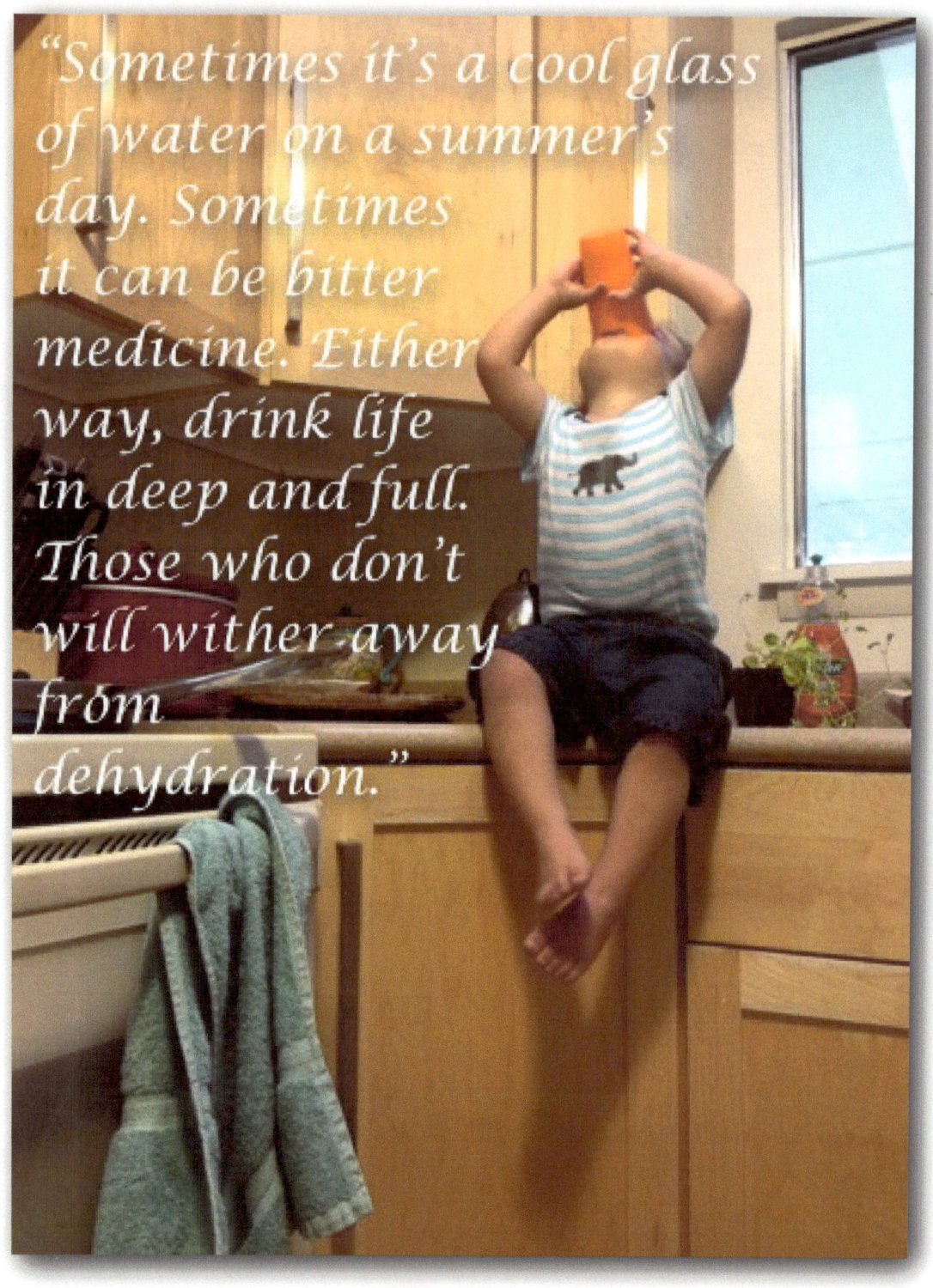

"Sometimes it's a cool glass of water on a summer's day. Sometimes it can be bitter medicine. Either way, drink life in deep and full. Those who don't will wither away from dehydration."

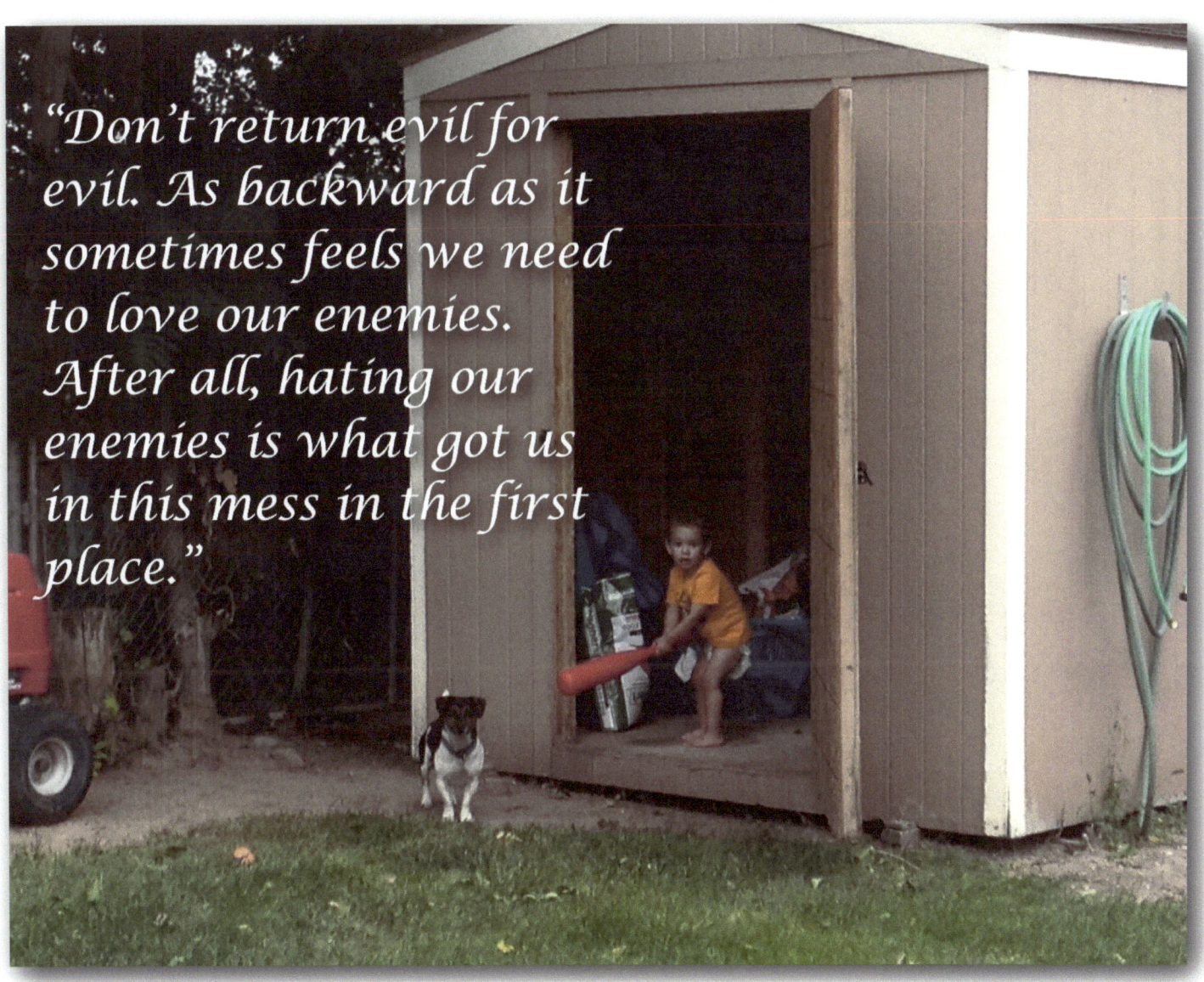

"Don't return evil for evil. As backward as it sometimes feels we need to love our enemies. After all, hating our enemies is what got us in this mess in the first place."

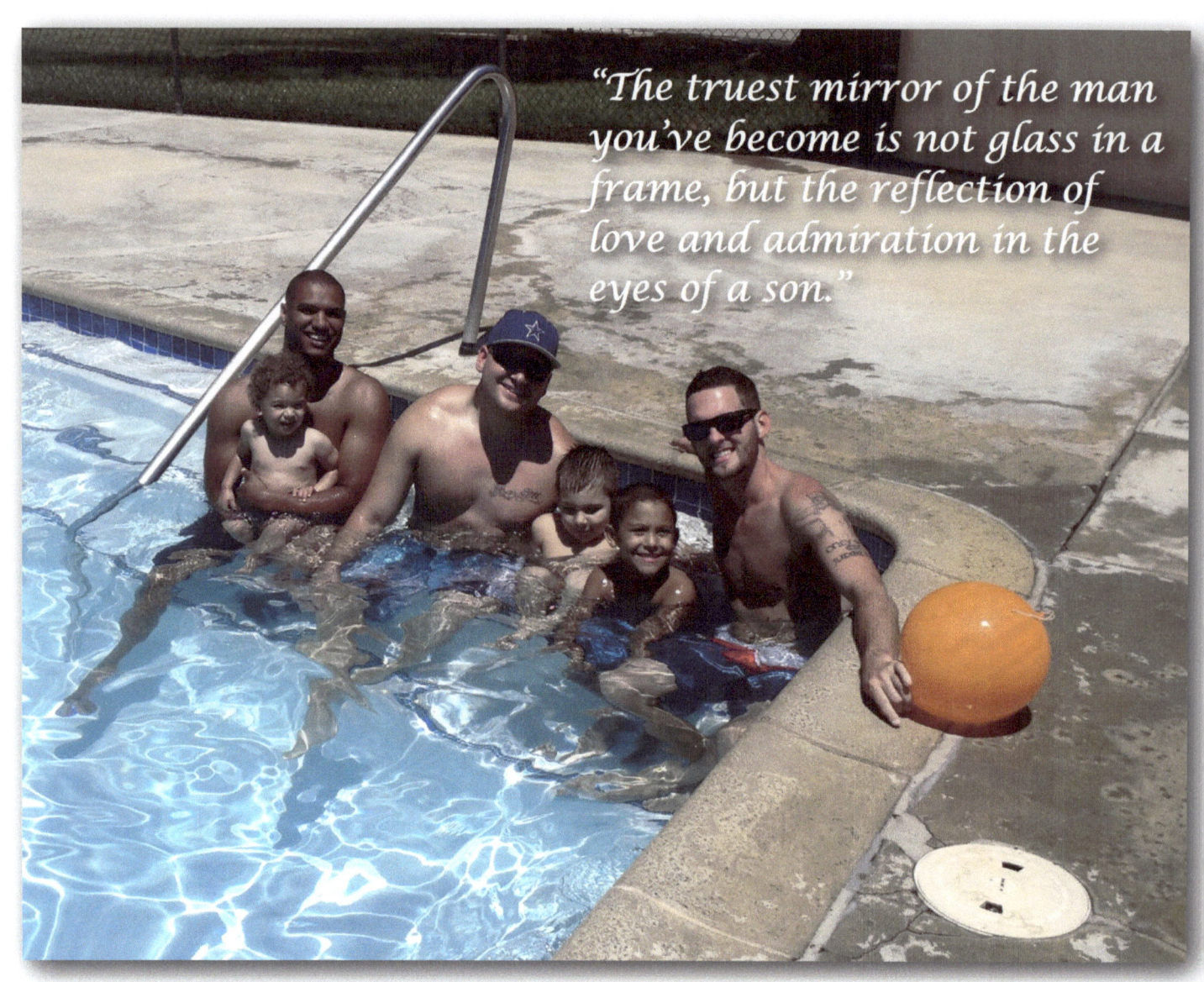

"The truest mirror of the man you've become is not glass in a frame, but the reflection of love and admiration in the eyes of a son."

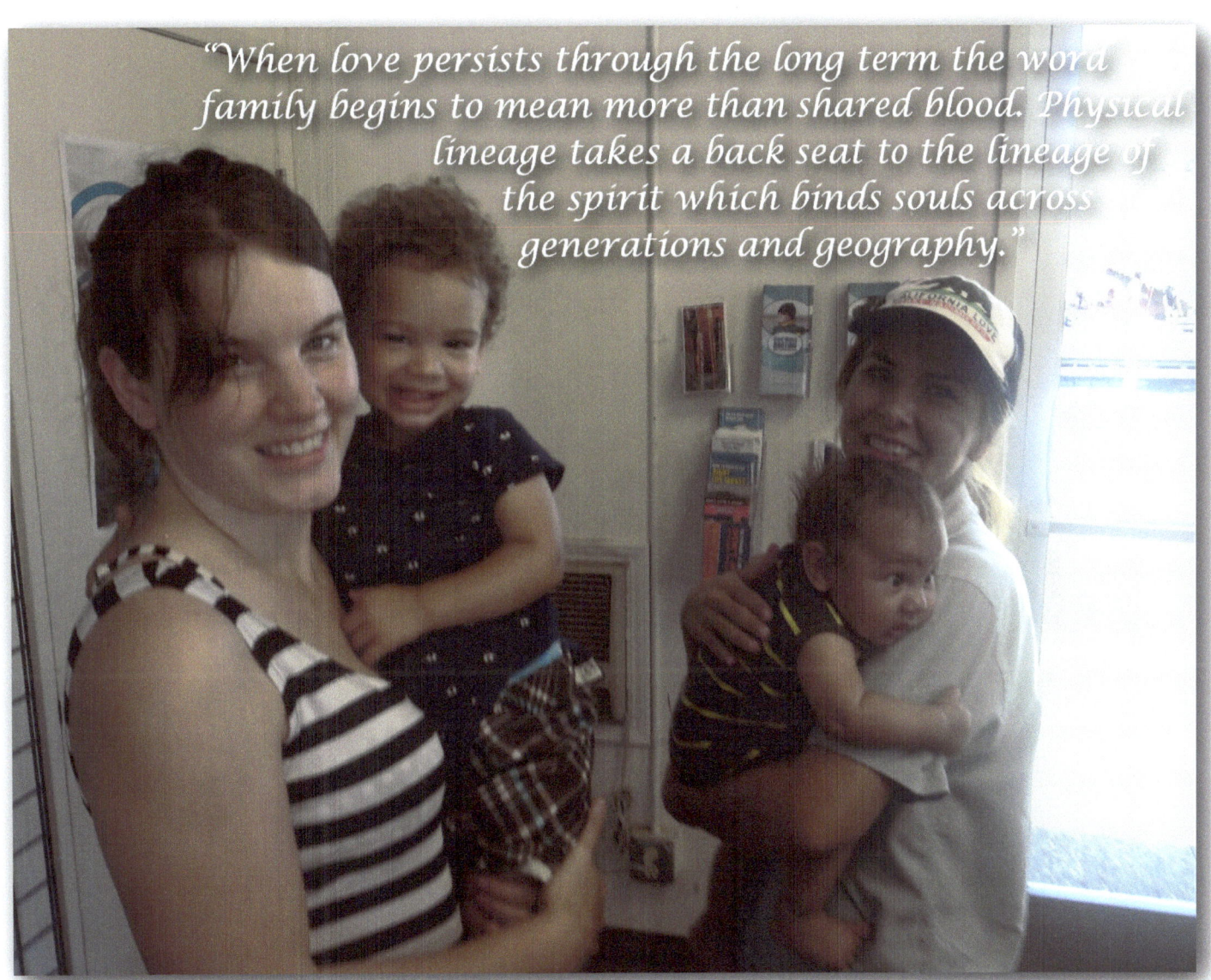

"When love persists through the long term the word family begins to mean more than shared blood. Physical lineage takes a back seat to the lineage of the spirit which binds souls across generations and geography."

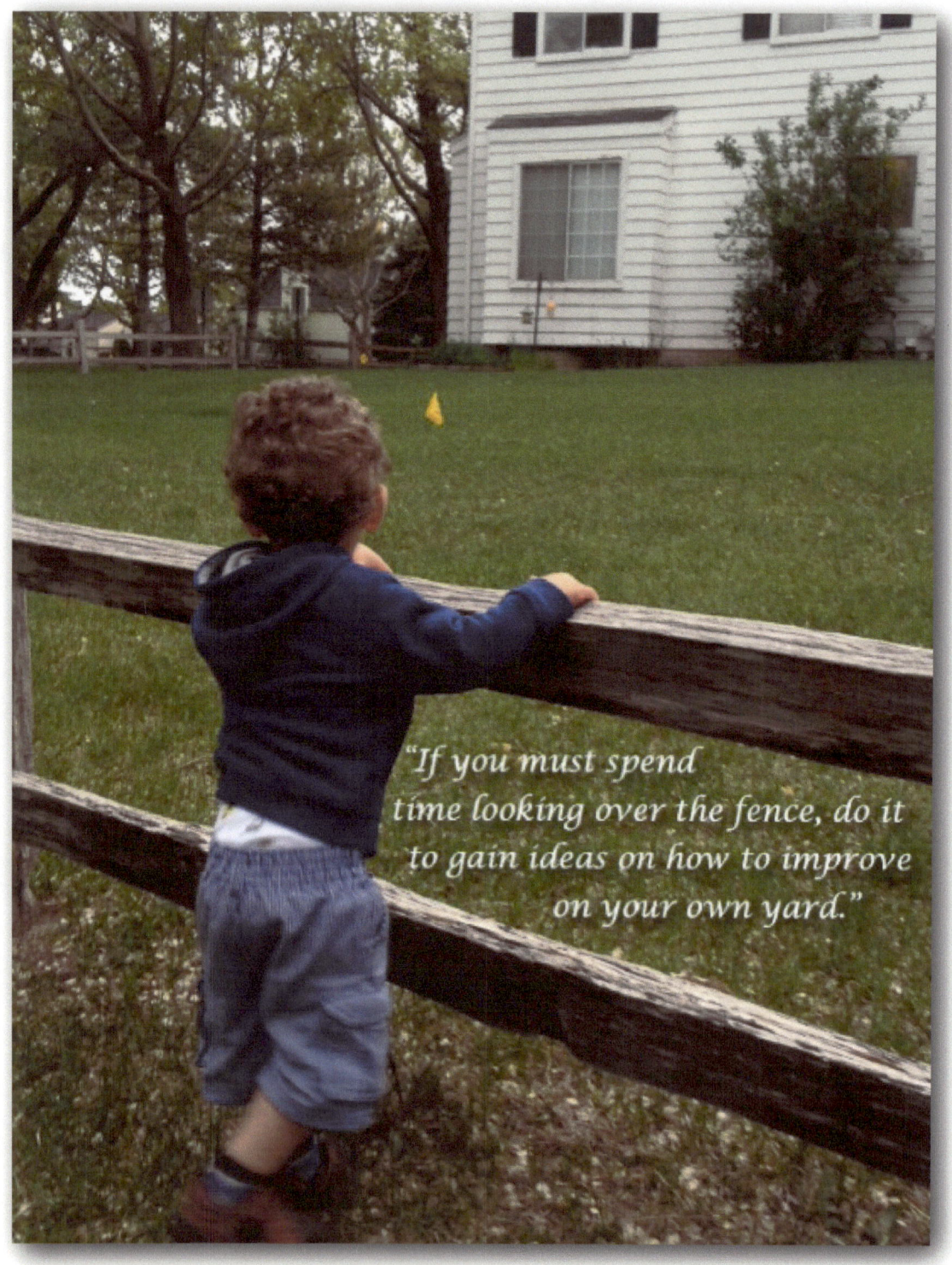

"If you must spend
time looking over the fence, do it
to gain ideas on how to improve
on your own yard."

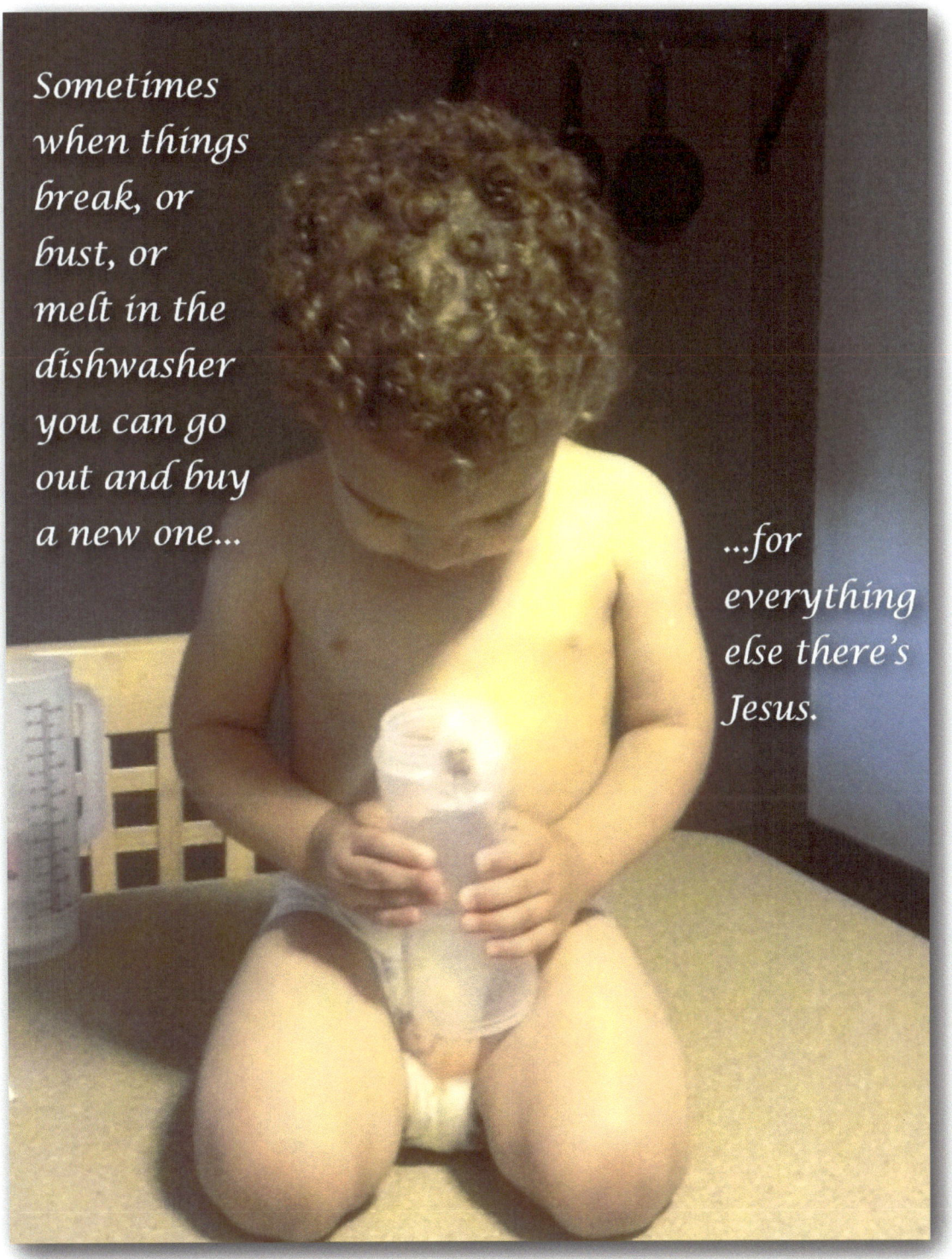

Sometimes when things break, or bust, or melt in the dishwasher you can go out and buy a new one...

...for everything else there's Jesus.

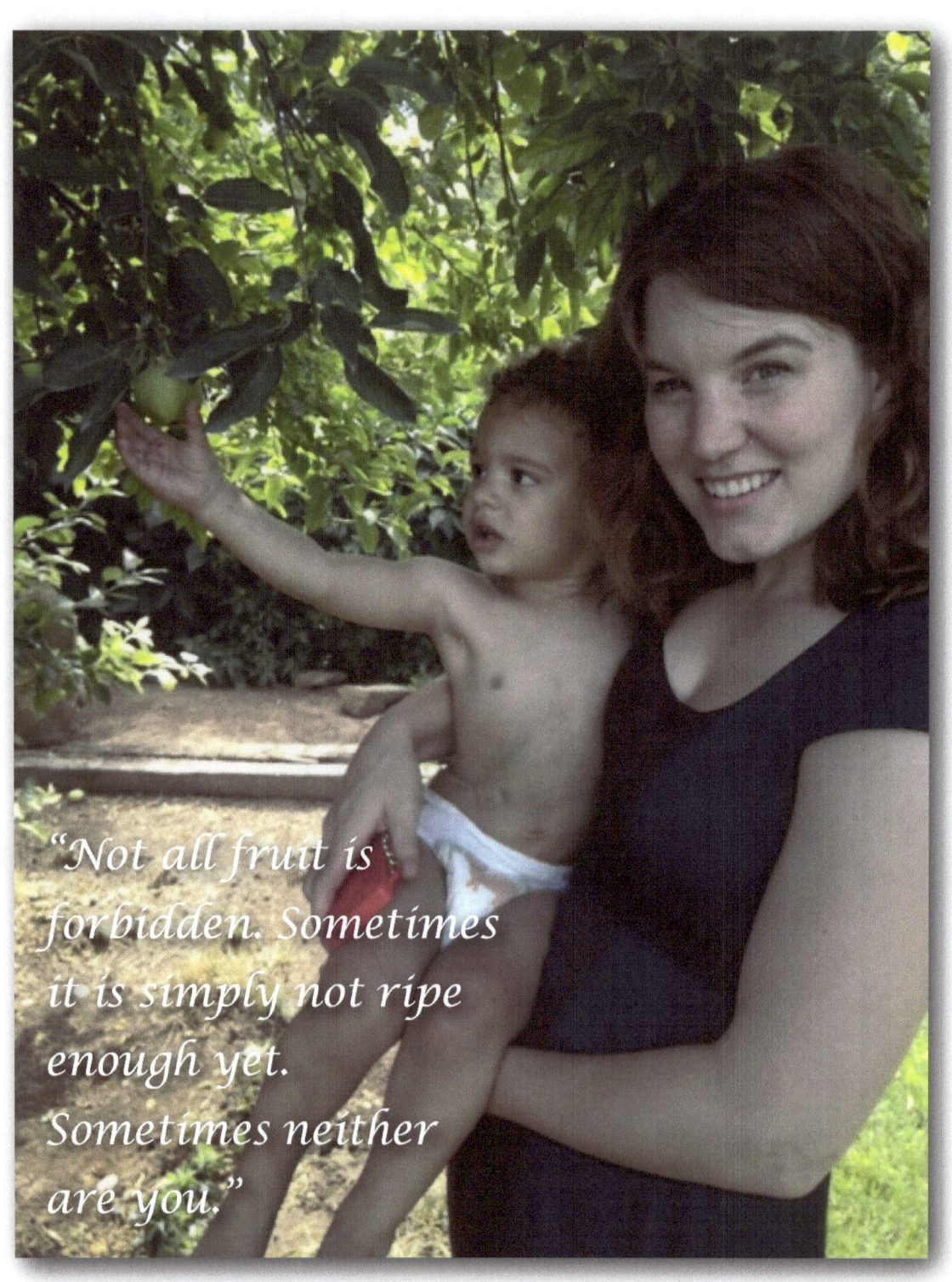

"Not all fruit is
forbidden. Sometimes
it is simply not ripe
enough yet.
Sometimes neither
are you."

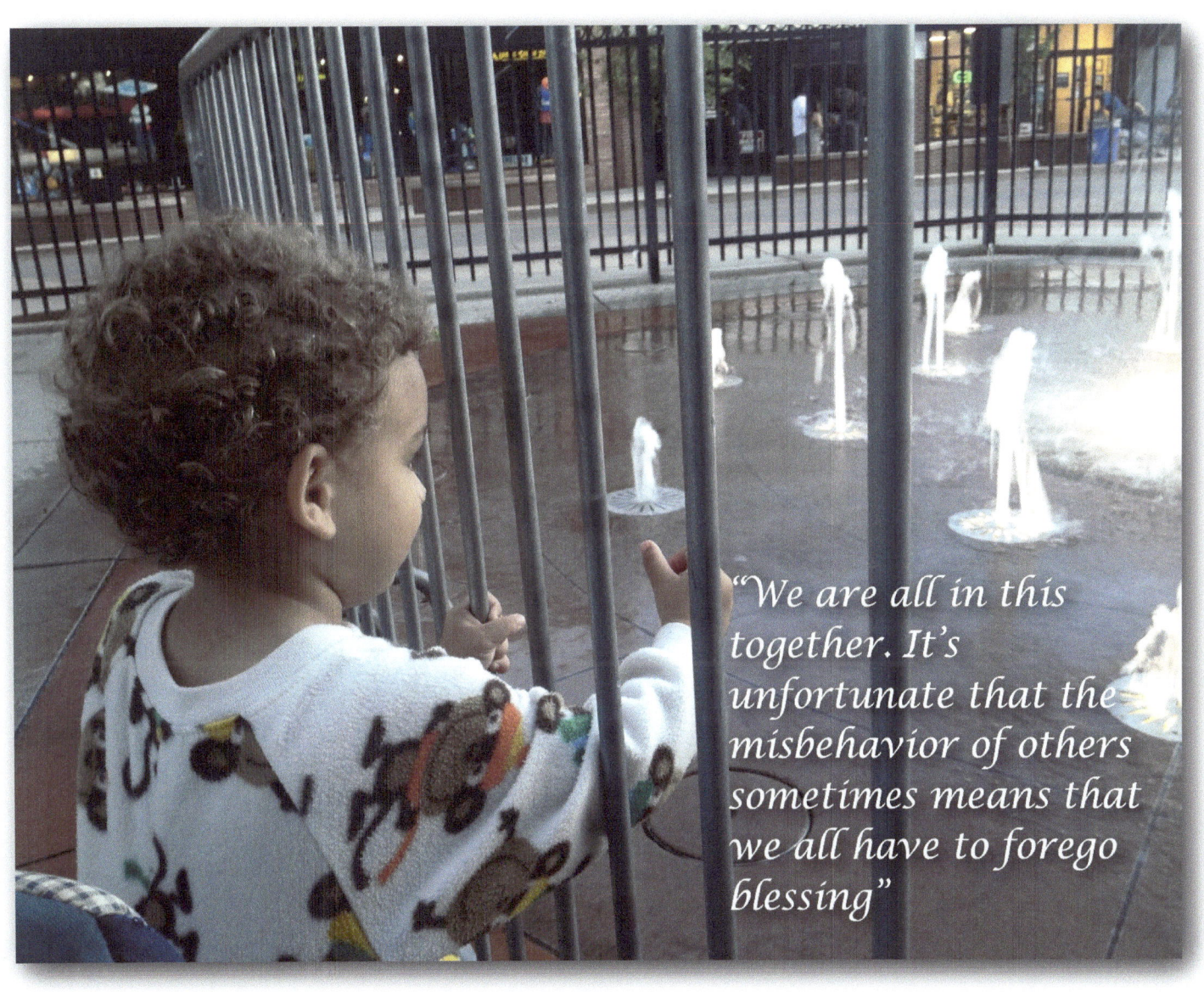

"We are all in this together. It's unfortunate that the misbehavior of others sometimes means that we all have to forego blessing"

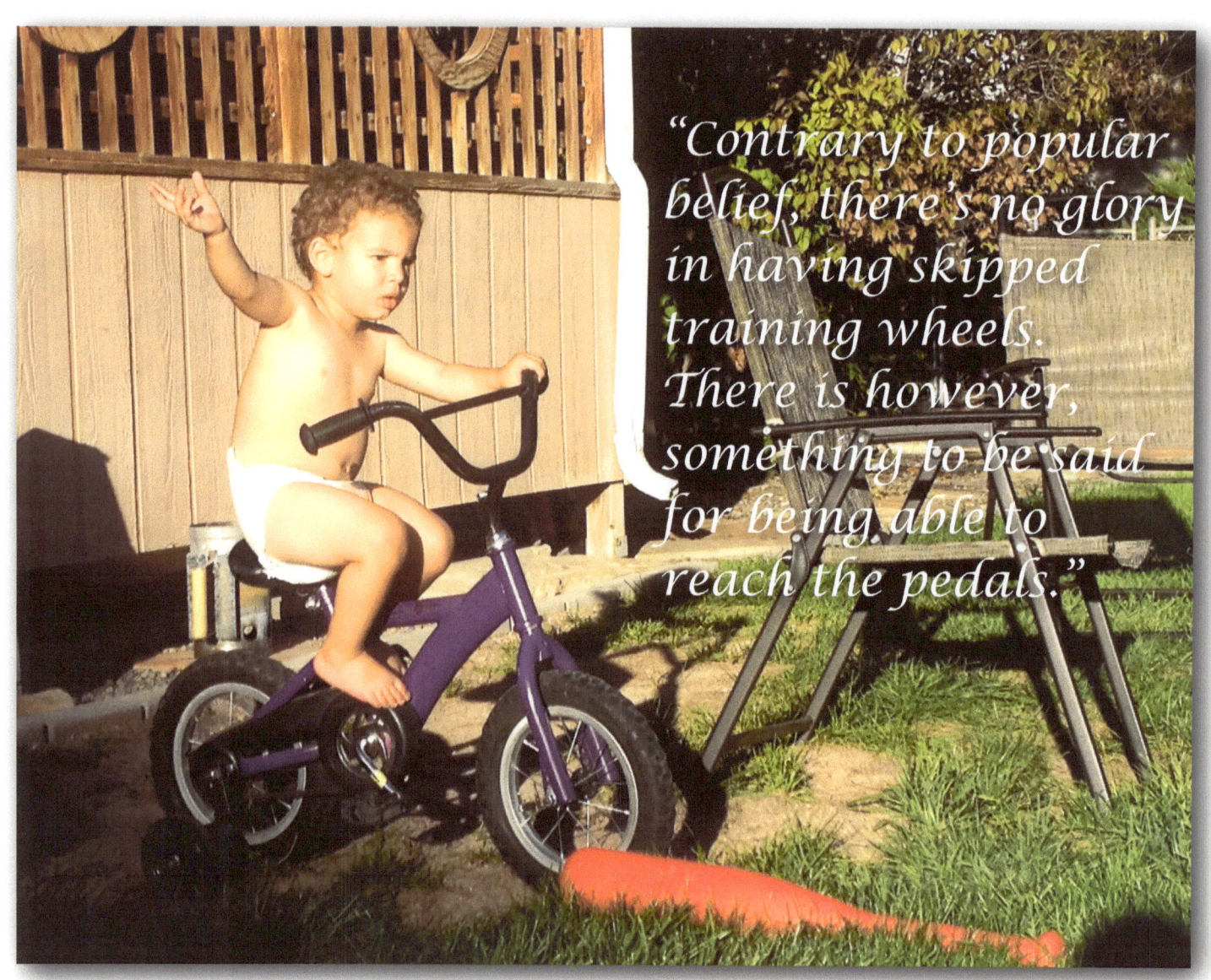

"Contrary to popular belief, there's no glory in having skipped training wheels. There is however, something to be said for being able to reach the pedals."

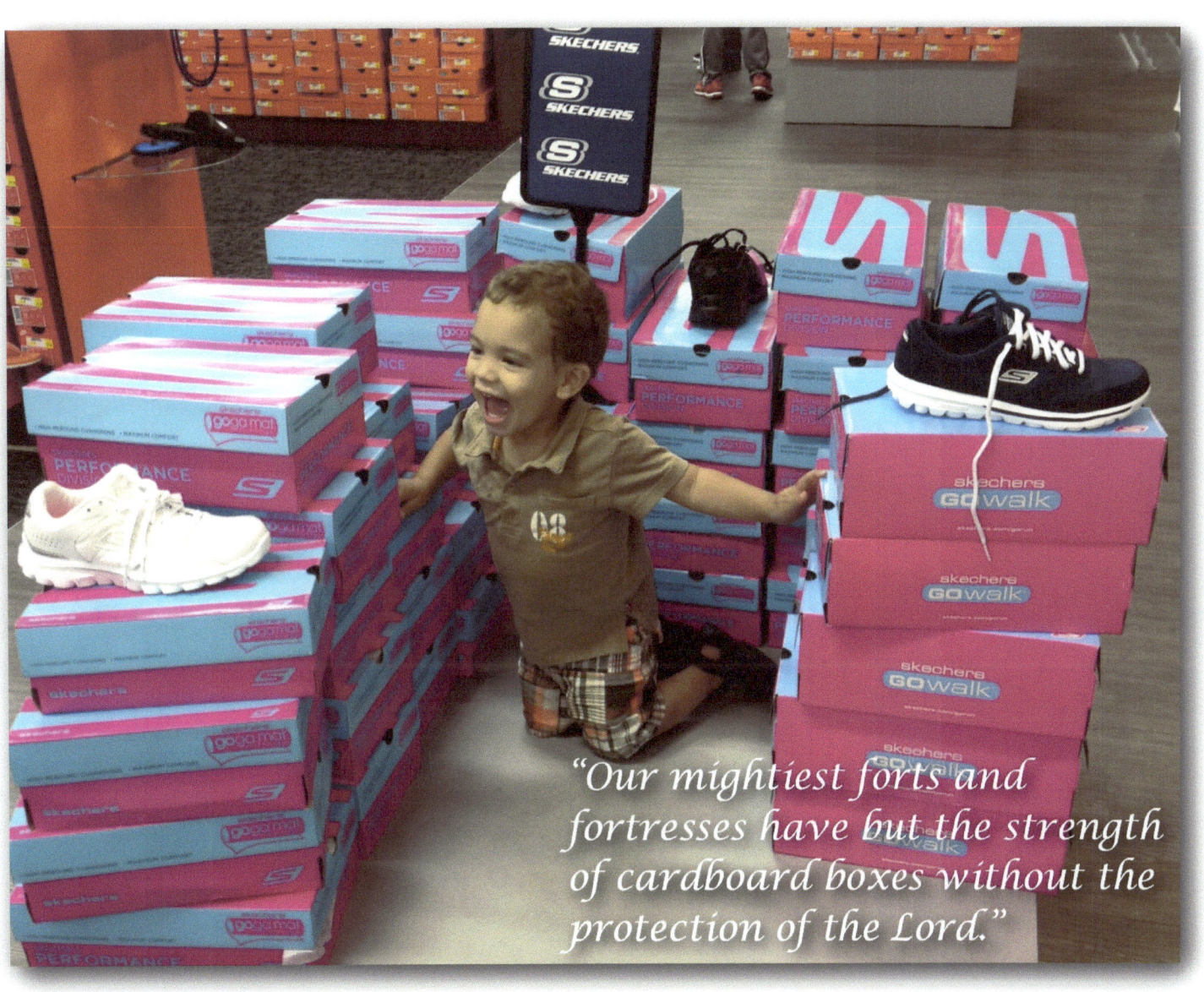

"Our mightiest forts and fortresses have but the strength of cardboard boxes without the protection of the Lord."

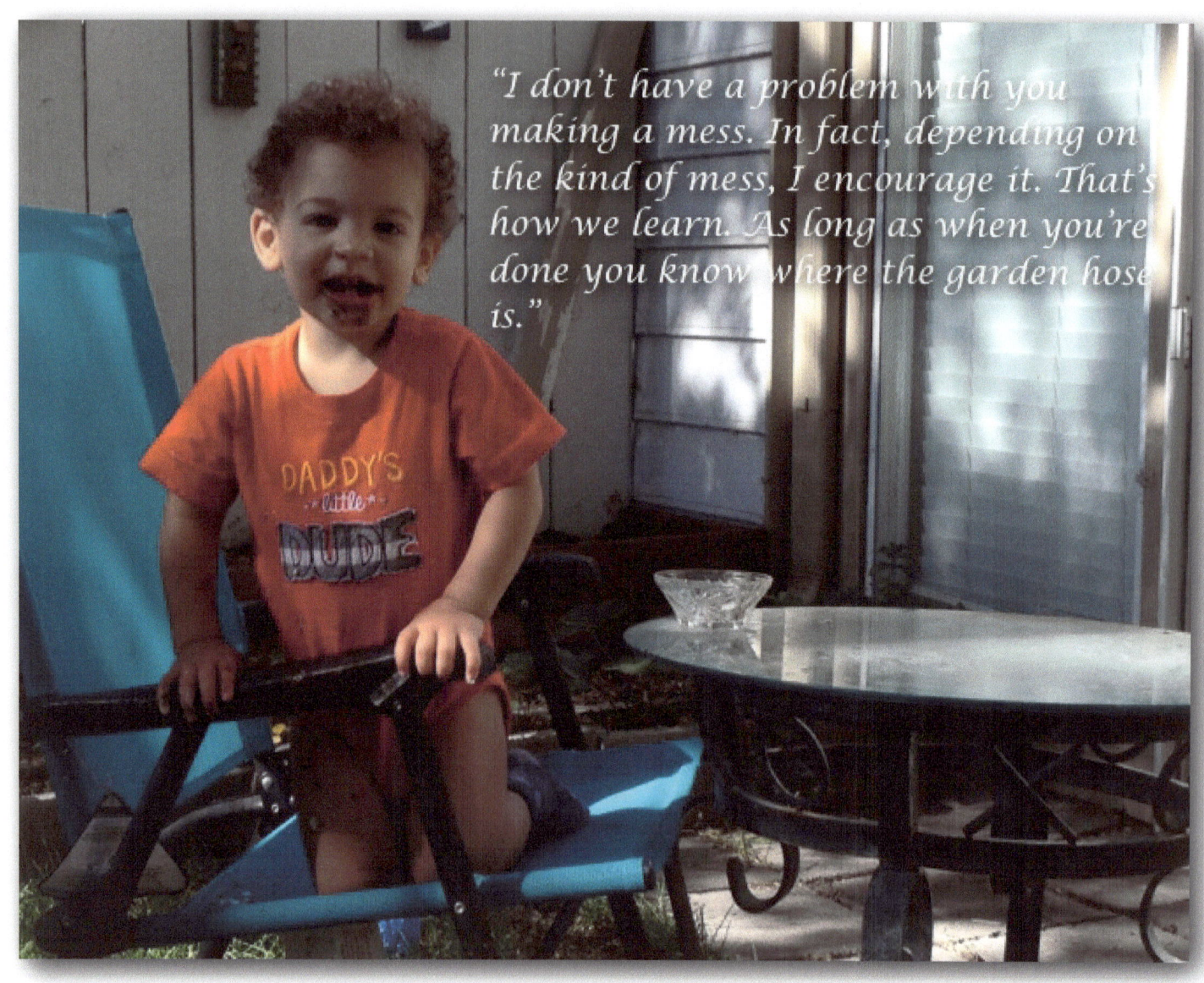

"I don't have a problem with you making a mess. In fact, depending on the kind of mess, I encourage it. That's how we learn. As long as when you're done you know where the garden hose is."

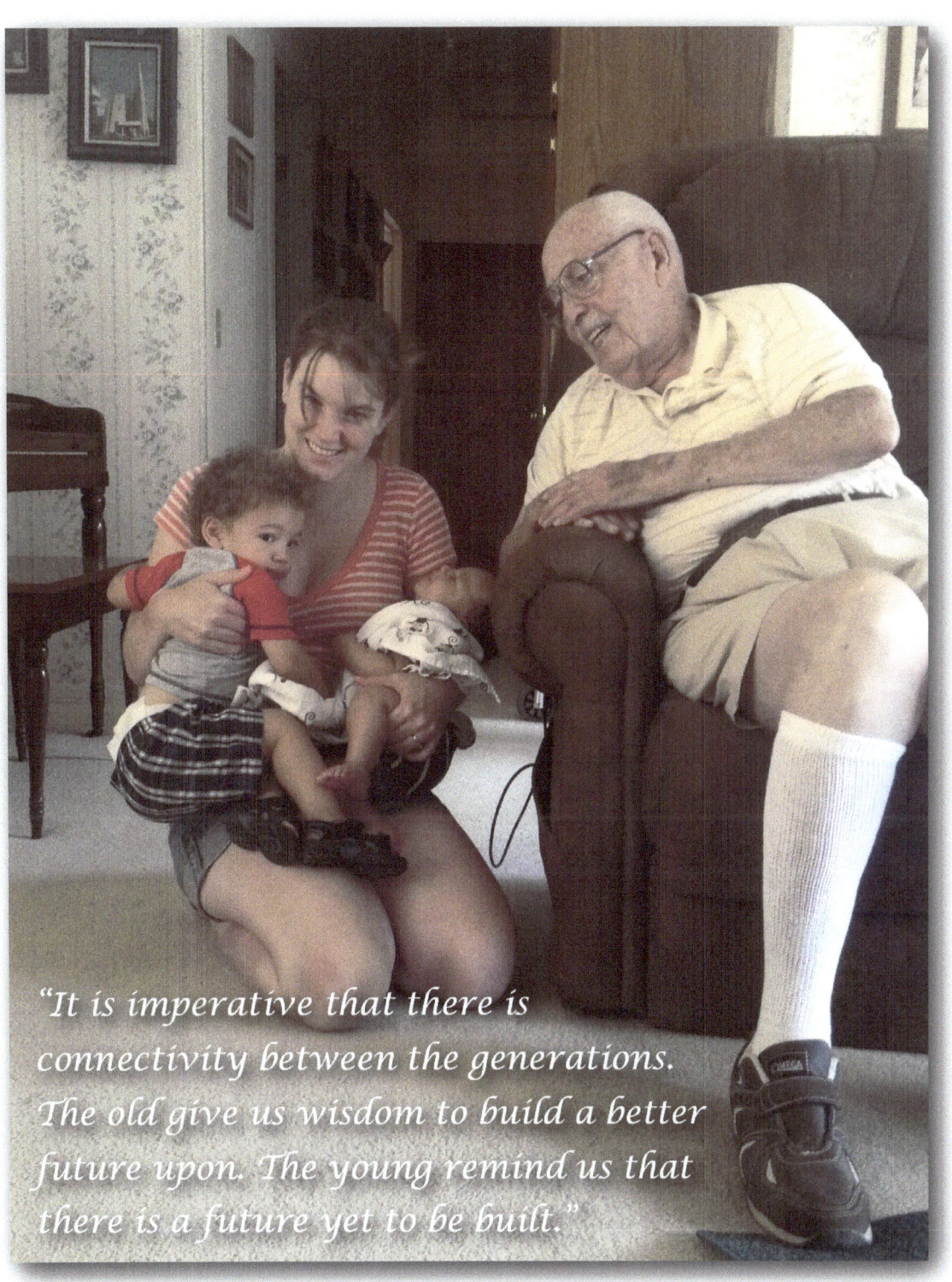

"It is imperative that there is connectivity between the generations. The old give us wisdom to build a better future upon. The young remind us that there is a future yet to be built."

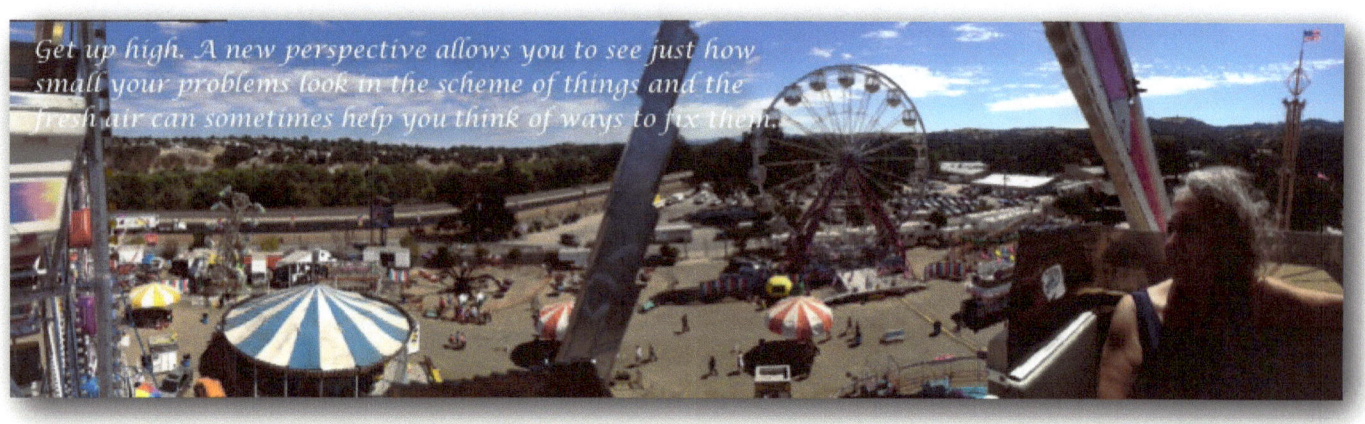

Get up high. A new perspective allows you to see just how small your problems look in the scheme of things and the fresh air can sometimes help you think of ways to fix them.

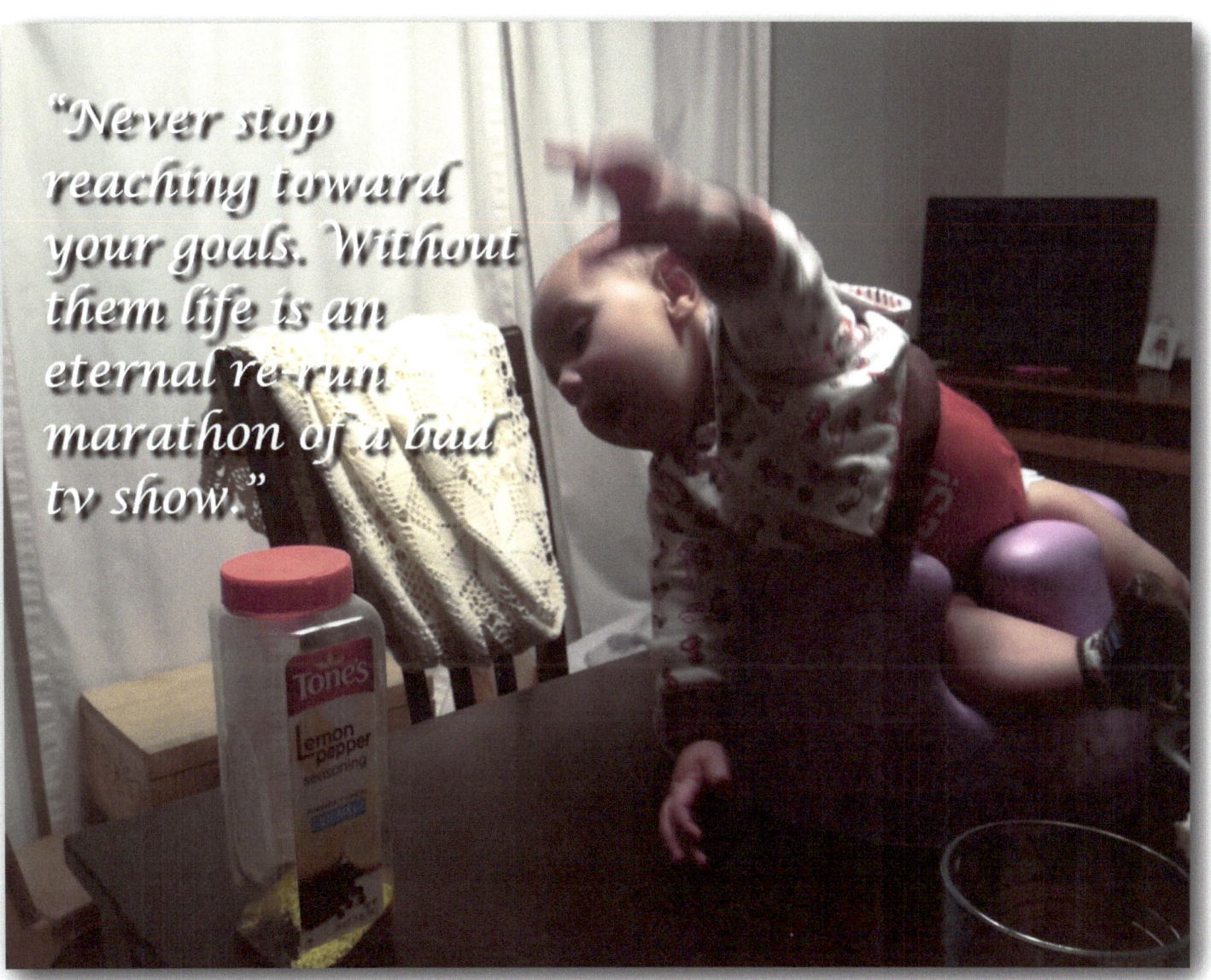

"Never stop reaching toward your goals. Without them life is an eternal re-run marathon of a bad tv show."

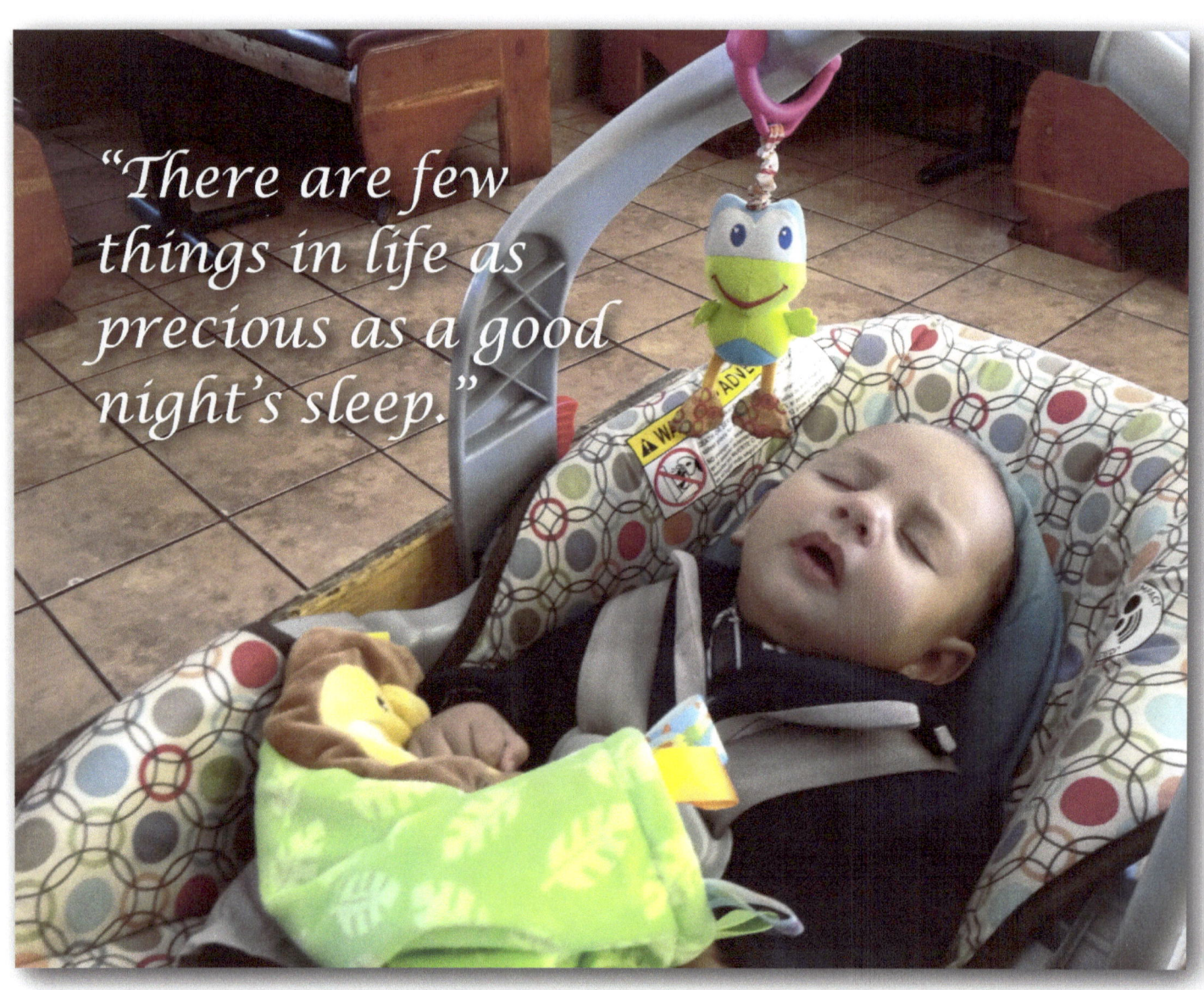

"There are few things in life as precious as a good night's sleep."

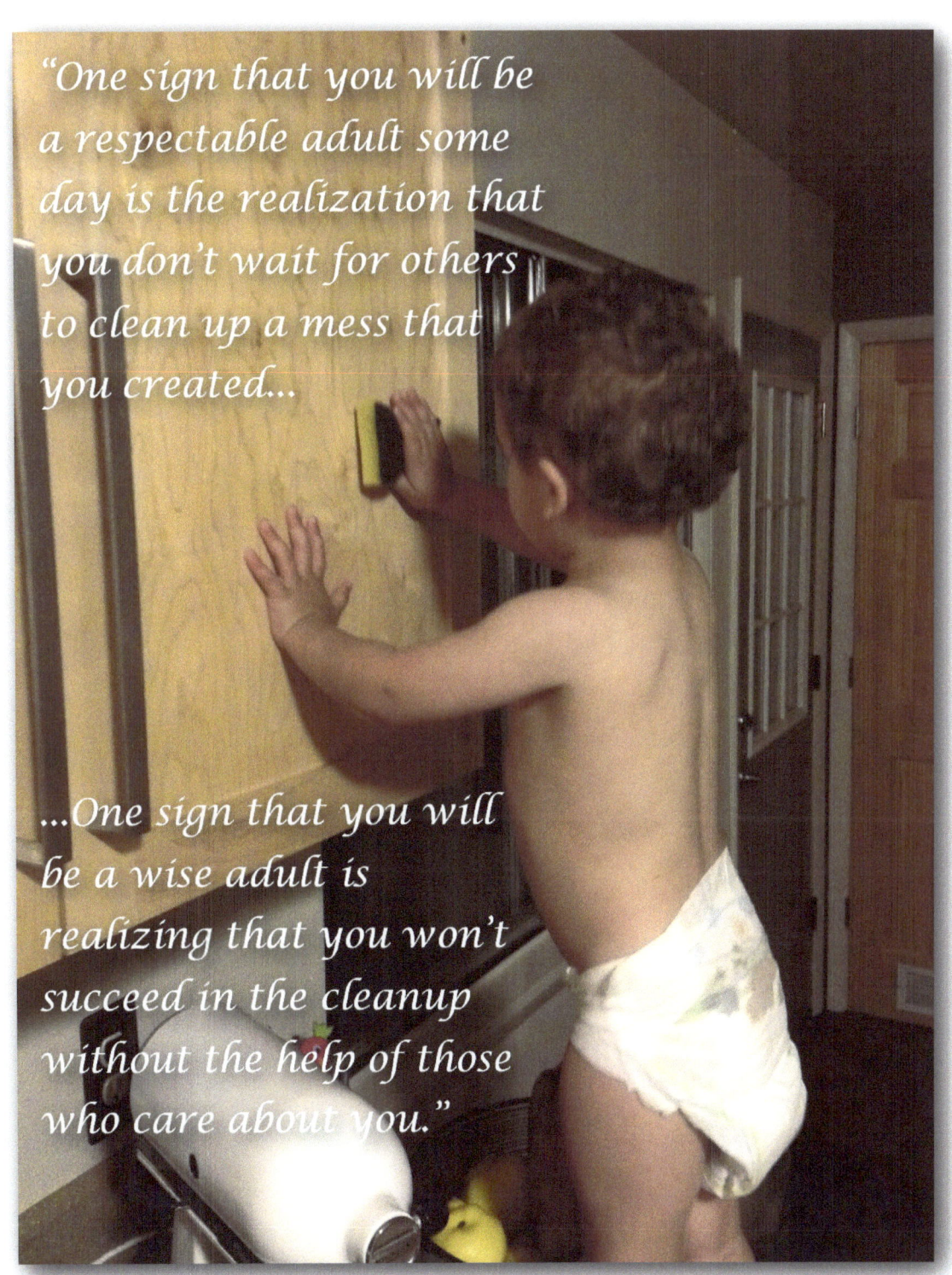

"One sign that you will be a respectable adult some day is the realization that you don't wait for others to clean up a mess that you created...

...One sign that you will be a wise adult is realizing that you won't succeed in the cleanup without the help of those who care about you."

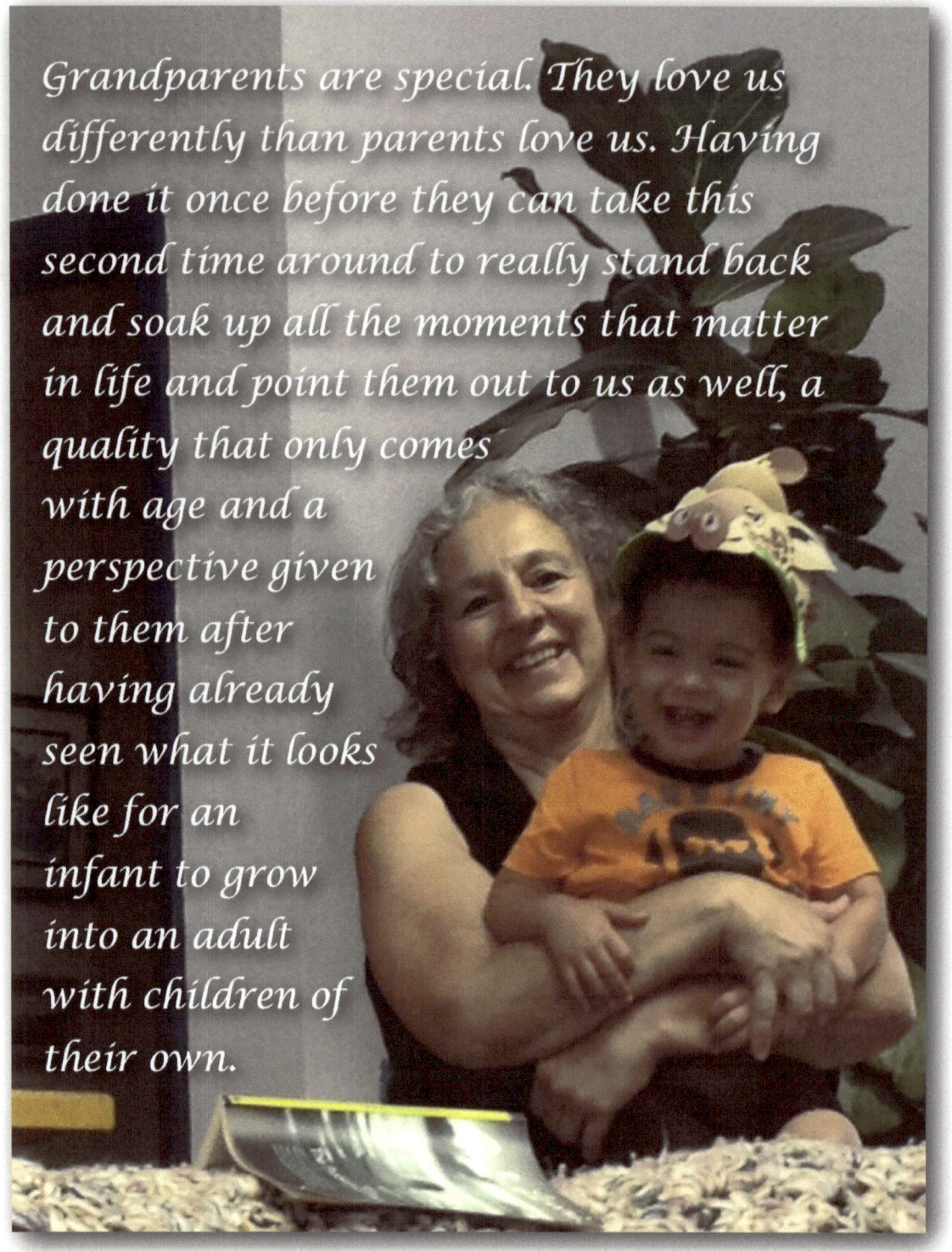

Grandparents are special. They love us differently than parents love us. Having done it once before they can take this second time around to really stand back and soak up all the moments that matter in life and point them out to us as well, a quality that only comes with age and a perspective given to them after having already seen what it looks like for an infant to grow into an adult with children of their own.

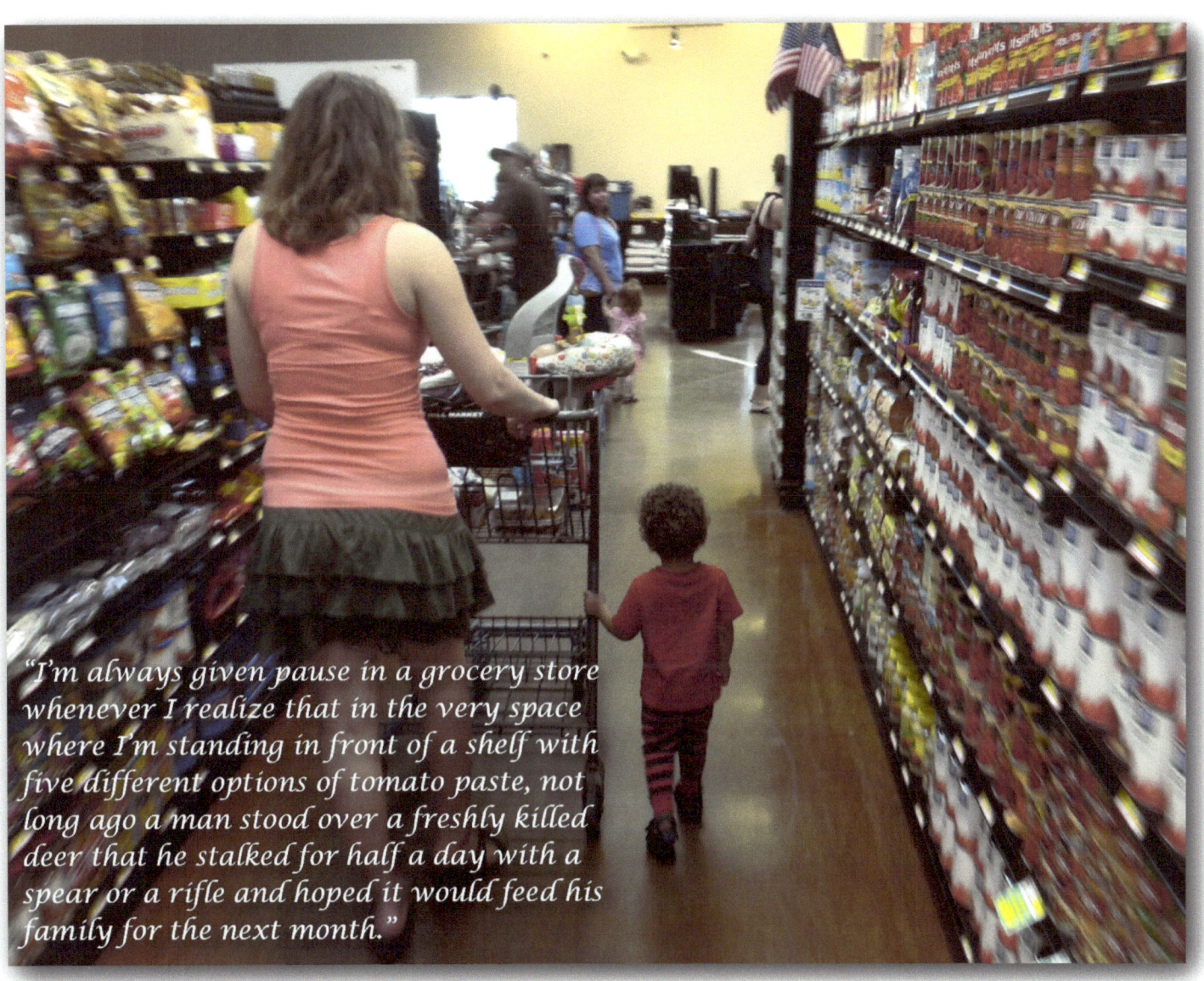

"I'm always given pause in a grocery store whenever I realize that in the very space where I'm standing in front of a shelf with five different options of tomato paste, not long ago a man stood over a freshly killed deer that he stalked for half a day with a spear or a rifle and hoped it would feed his family for the next month."

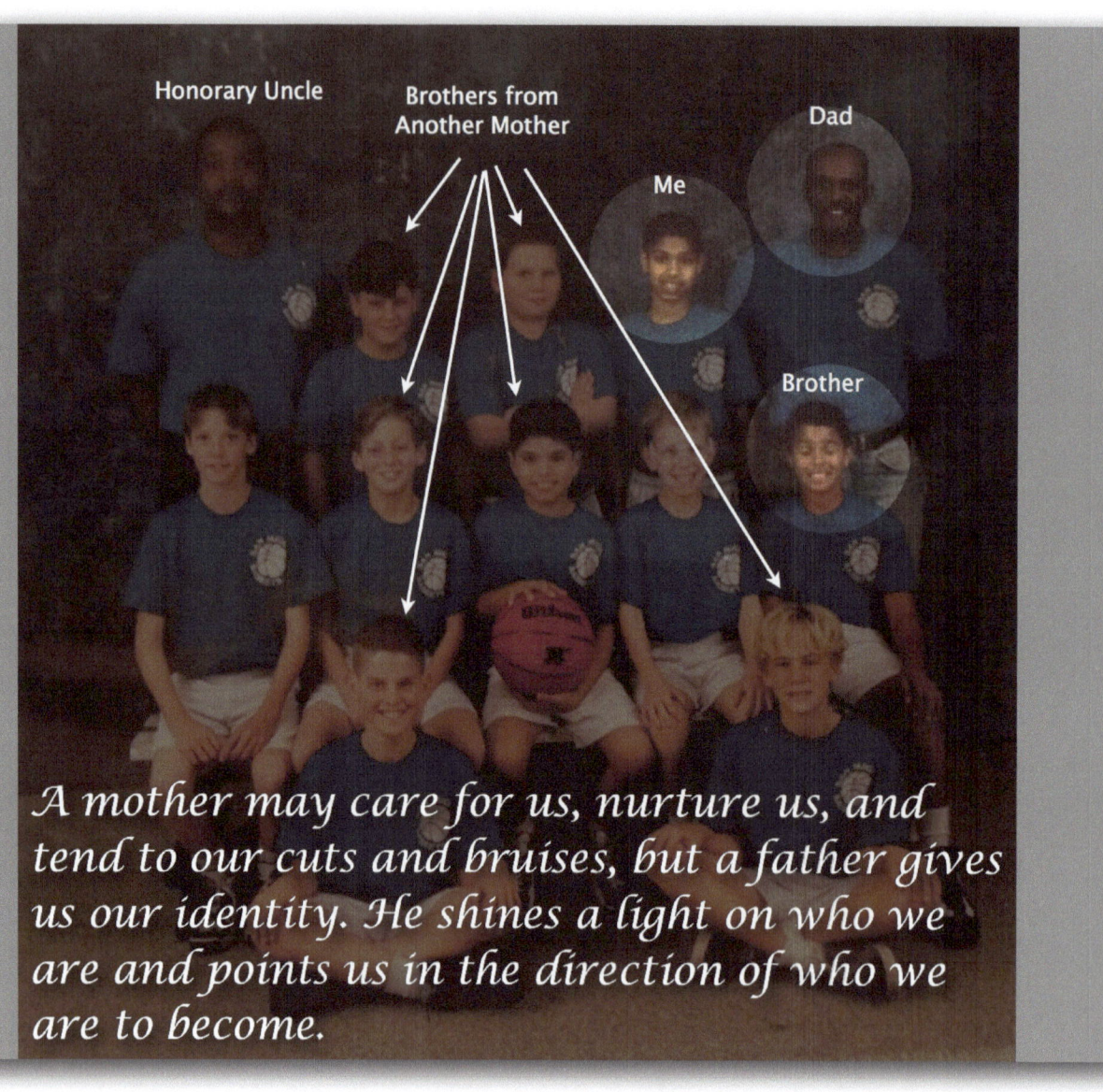

Honorary Uncle

Brothers from
Another Mother

Dad

Me

Brother

A mother may care for us, nurture us, and tend to our cuts and bruises, but a father gives us our identity. He shines a light on who we are and points us in the direction of who we are to become.

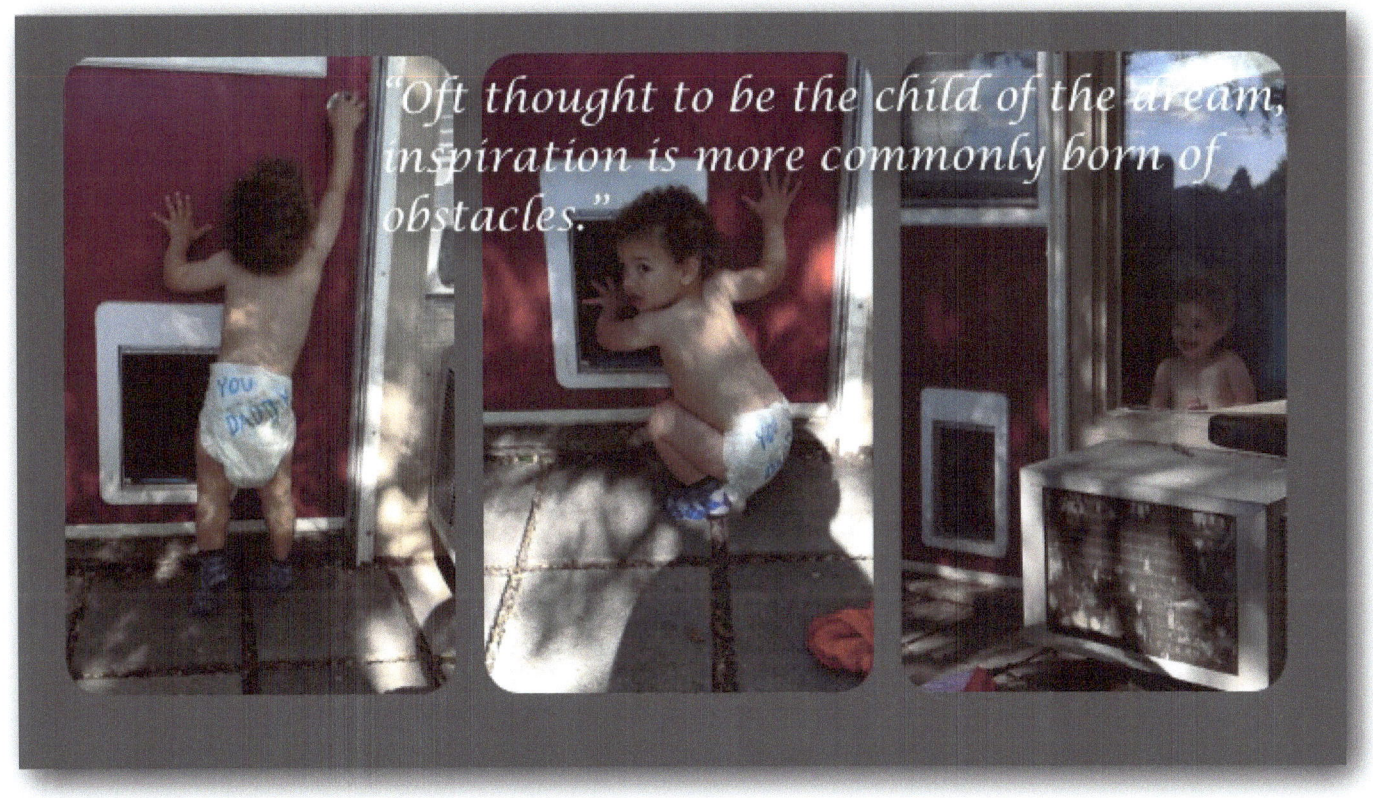

"Oft thought to be the child of the dream, inspiration is more commonly born of obstacles."

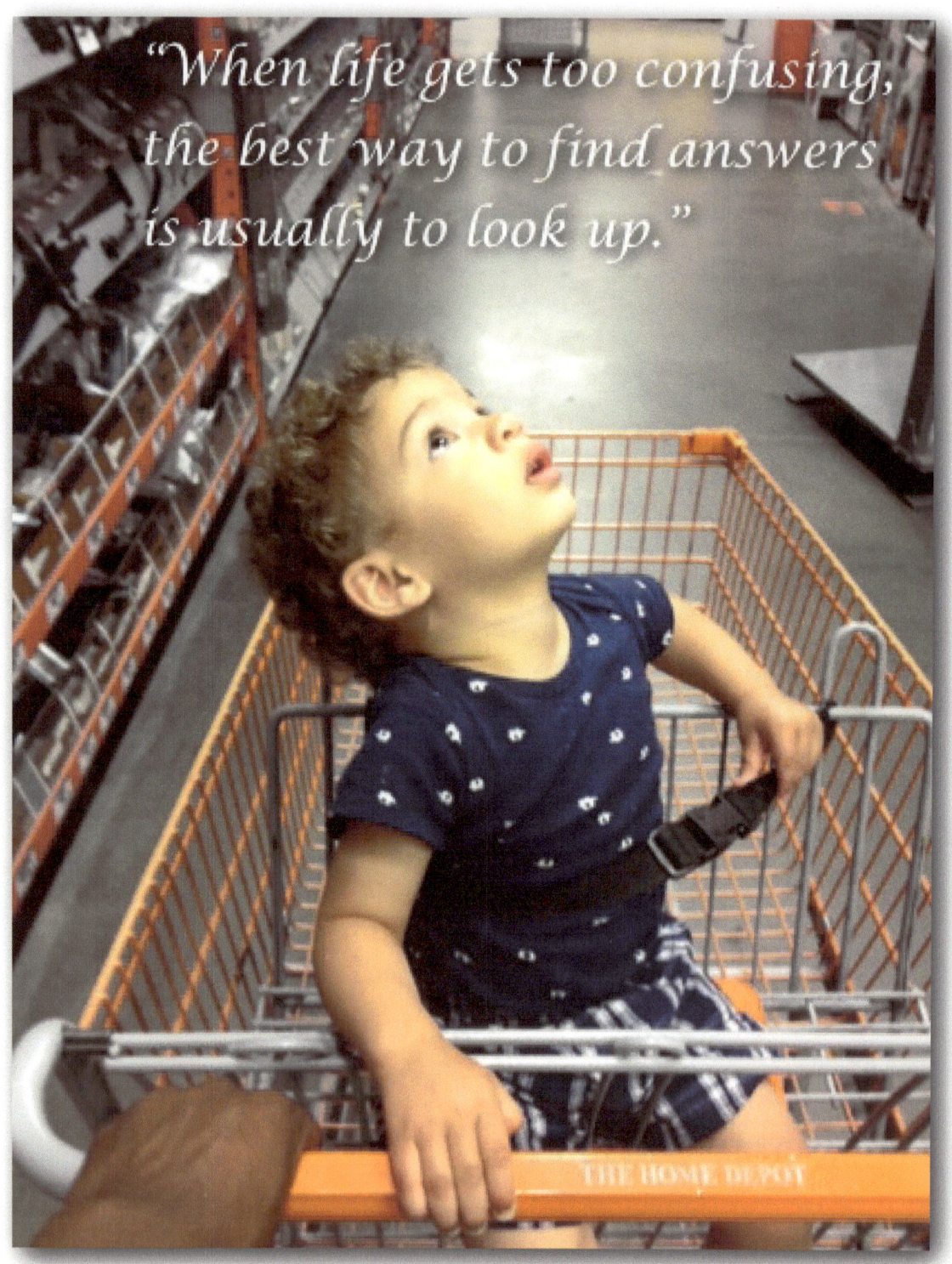

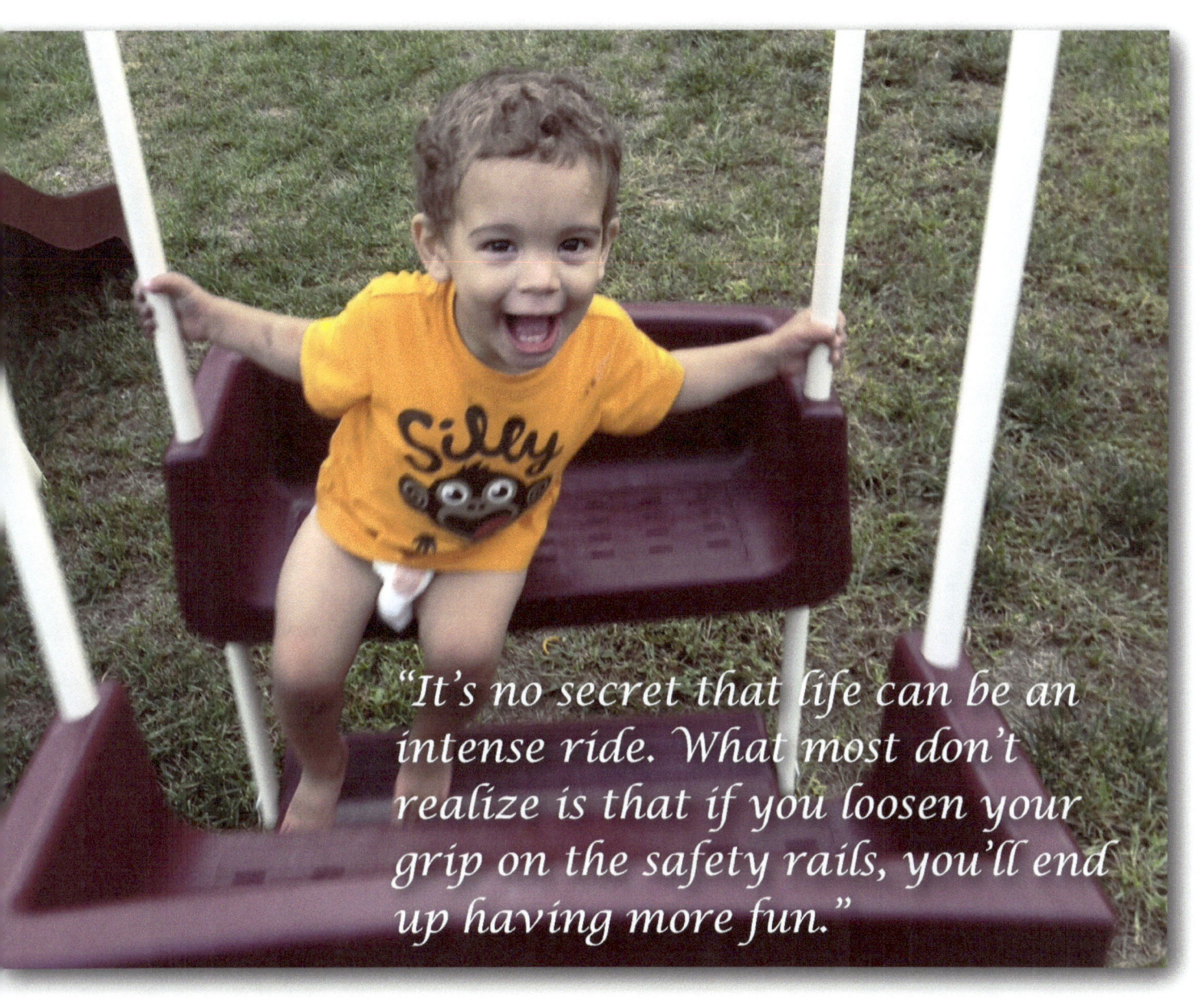

"It's no secret that life can be an intense ride. What most don't realize is that if you loosen your grip on the safety rails, you'll end up having more fun."

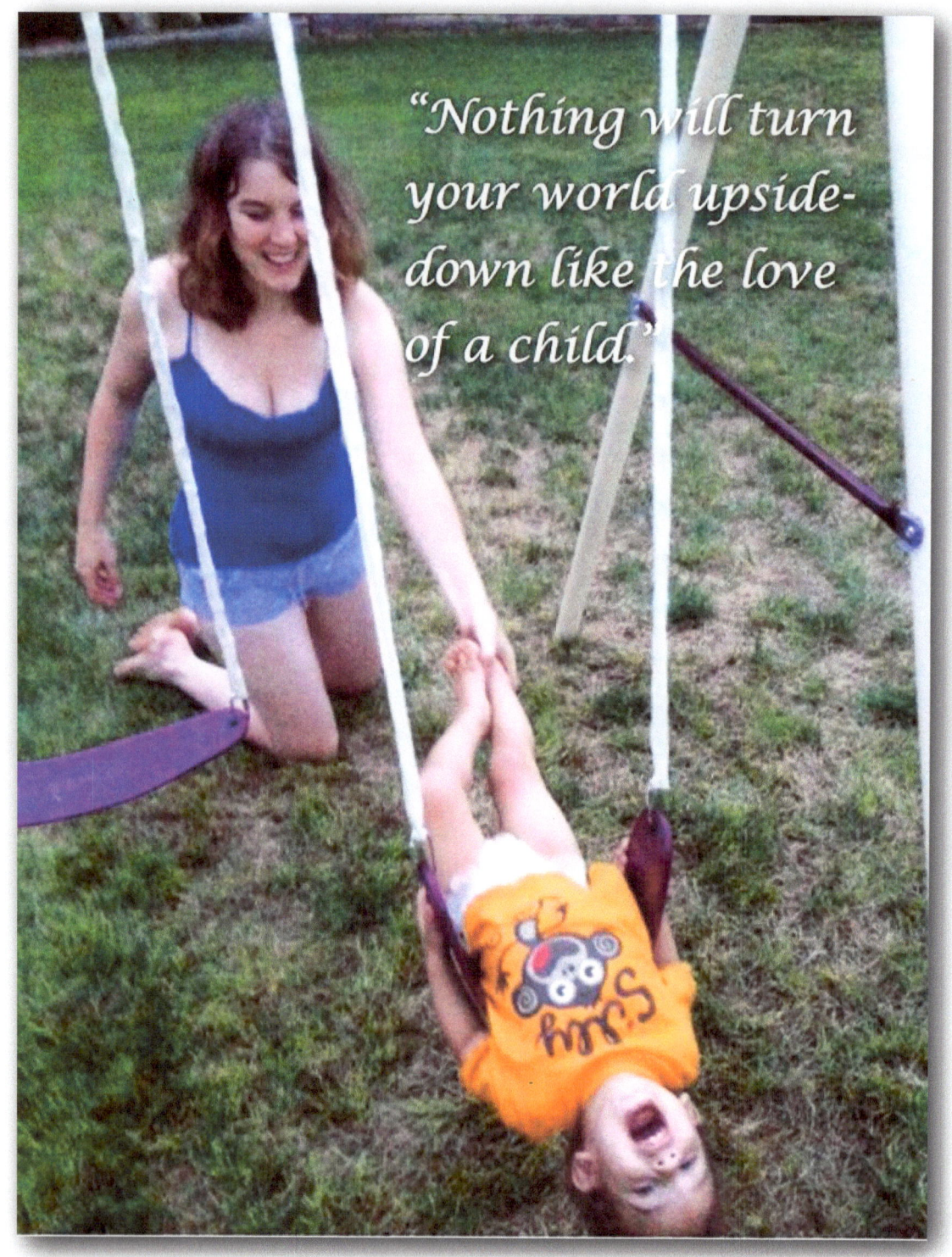

"Nothing will turn your world upside-down like the love of a child."

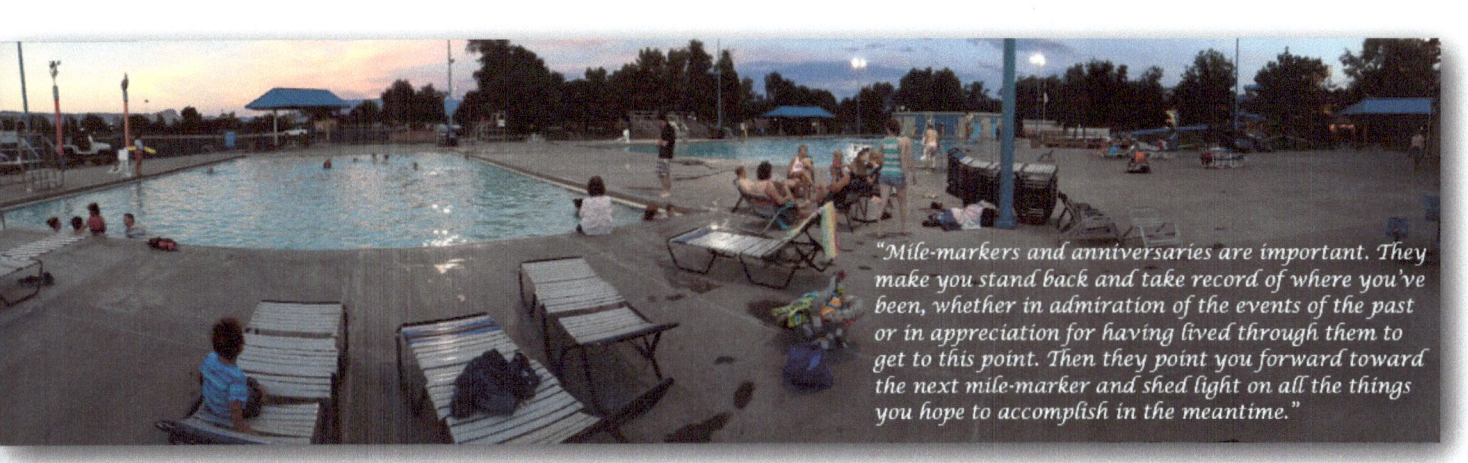

"Mile-markers and anniversaries are important. They make you stand back and take record of where you've been, whether in admiration of the events of the past or in appreciation for having lived through them to get to this point. Then they point you forward toward the next mile-marker and shed light on all the things you hope to accomplish in the meantime."

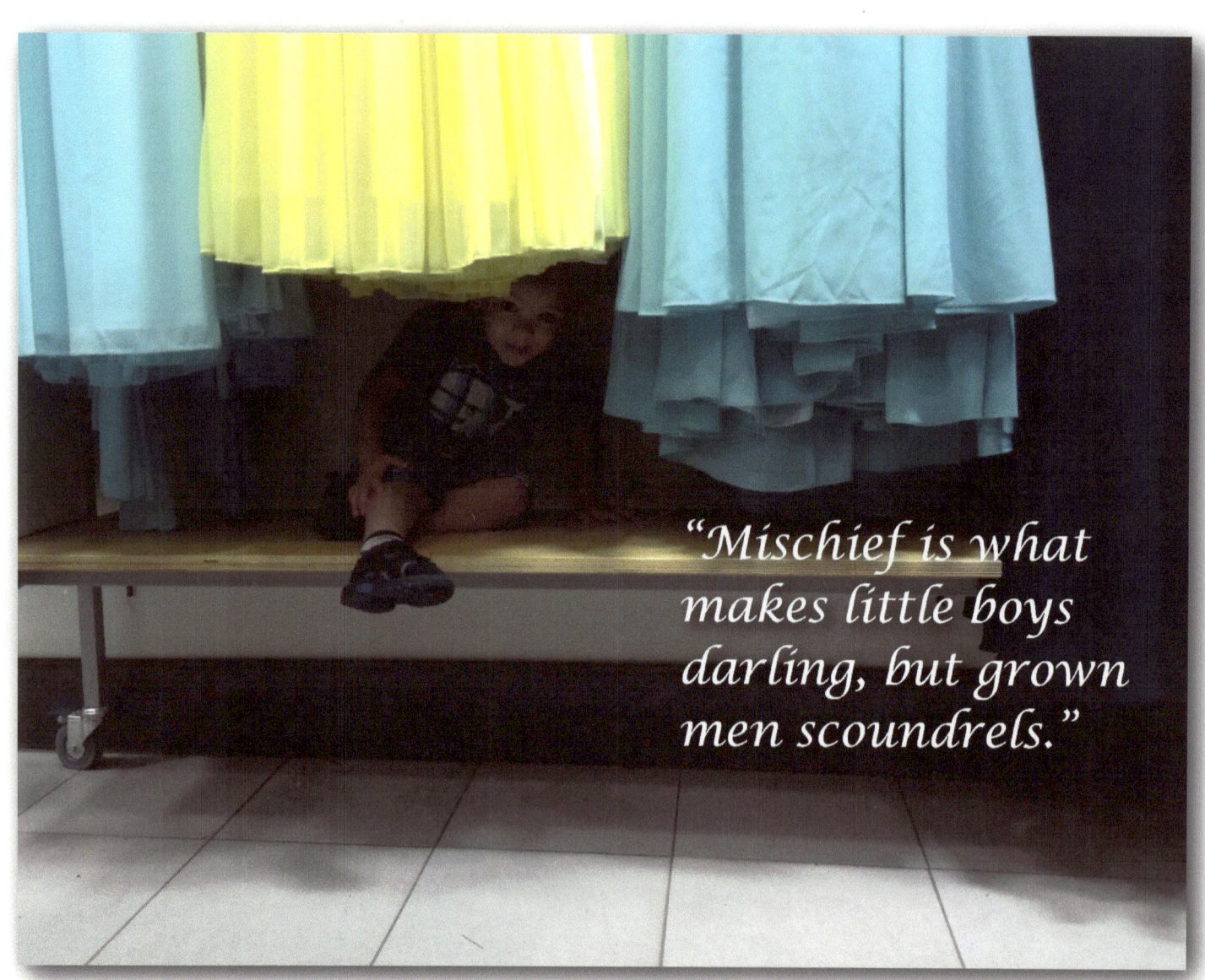

"Mischief is what makes little boys darling, but grown men scoundrels."

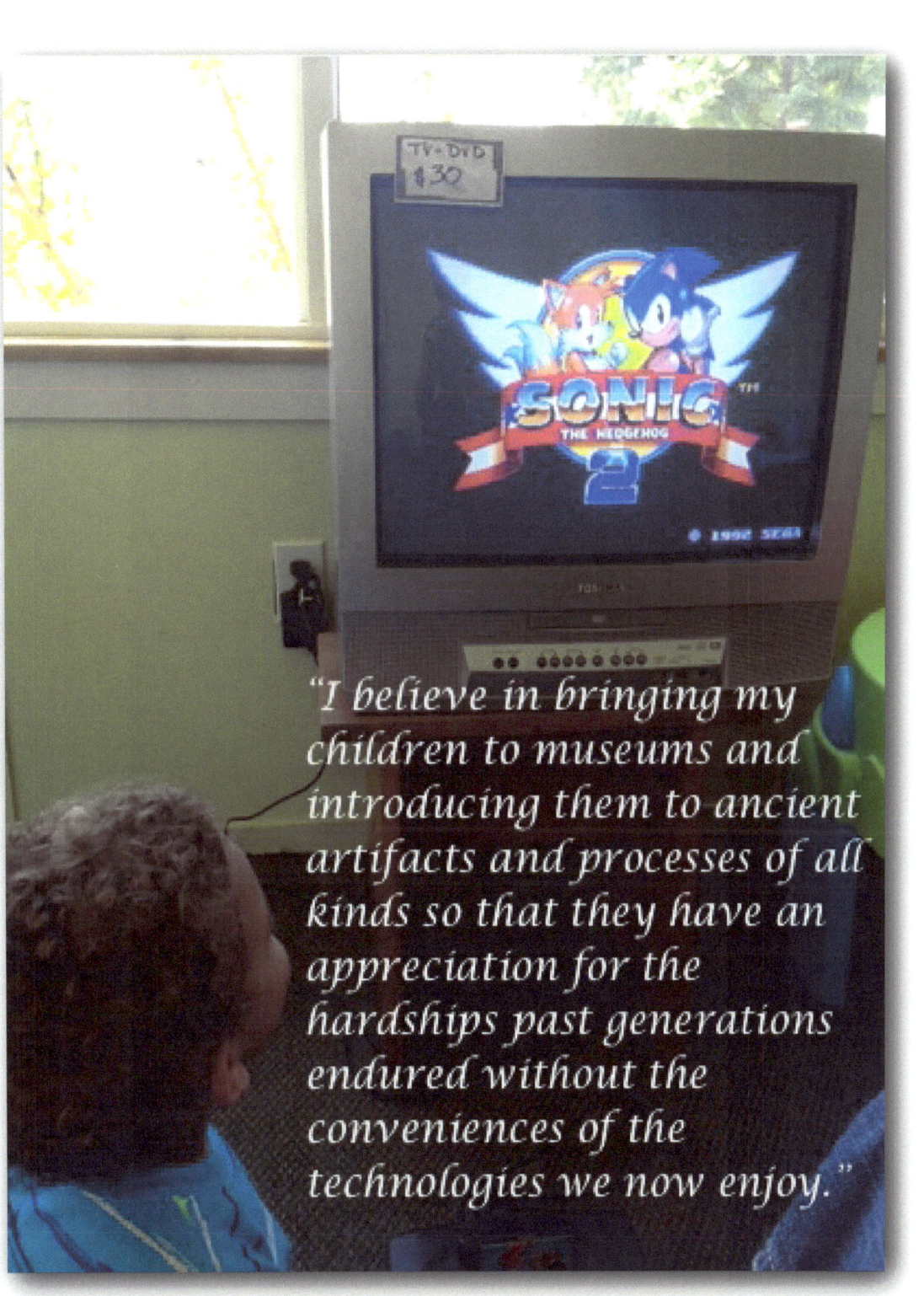

"I believe in bringing my children to museums and introducing them to ancient artifacts and processes of all kinds so that they have an appreciation for the hardships past generations endured without the conveniences of the technologies we now enjoy."

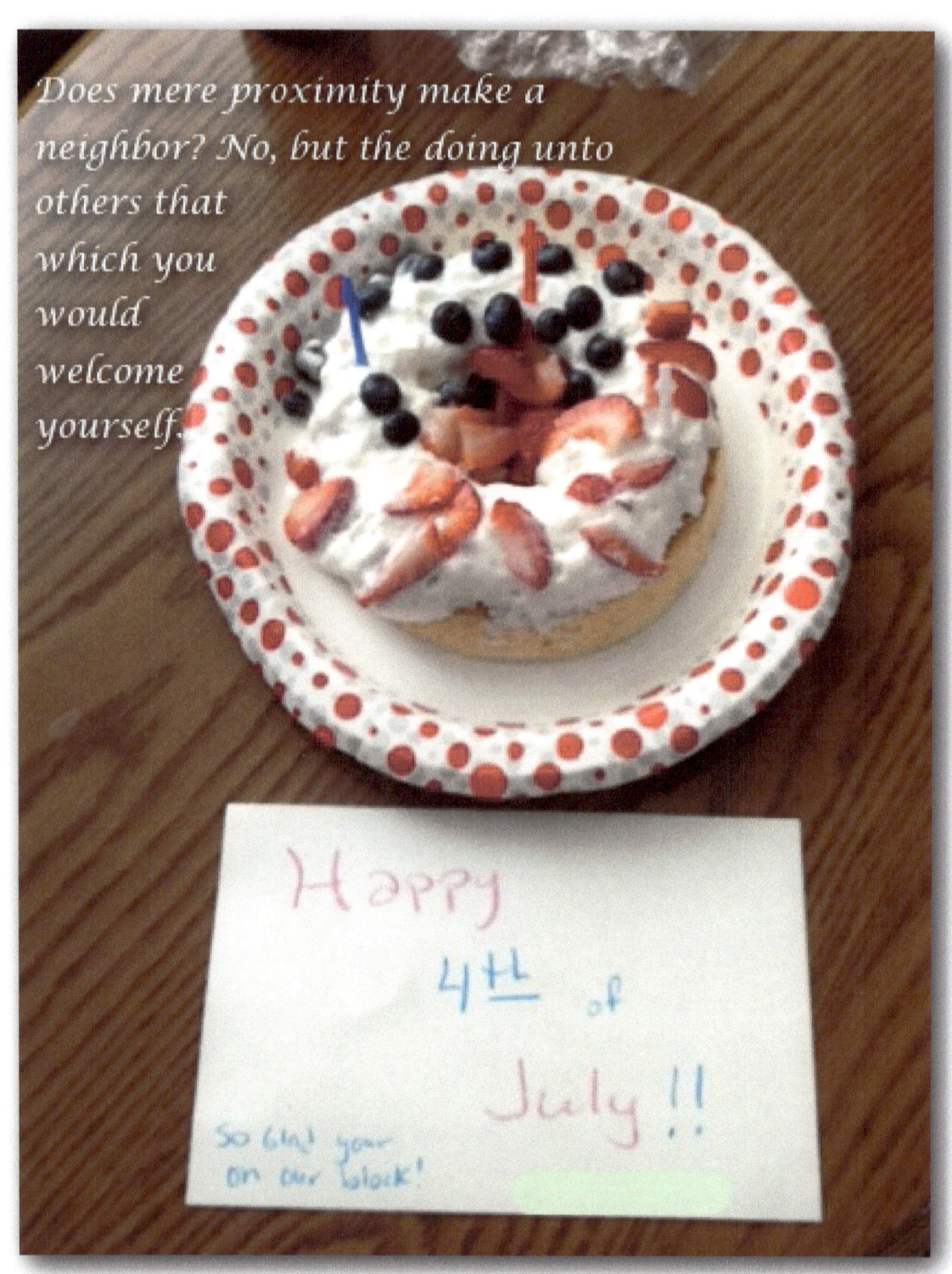

Does mere proximity make a neighbor? No, but the doing unto others that which you would welcome yourself.

Happy 4th of July !!

So glad your on our block!

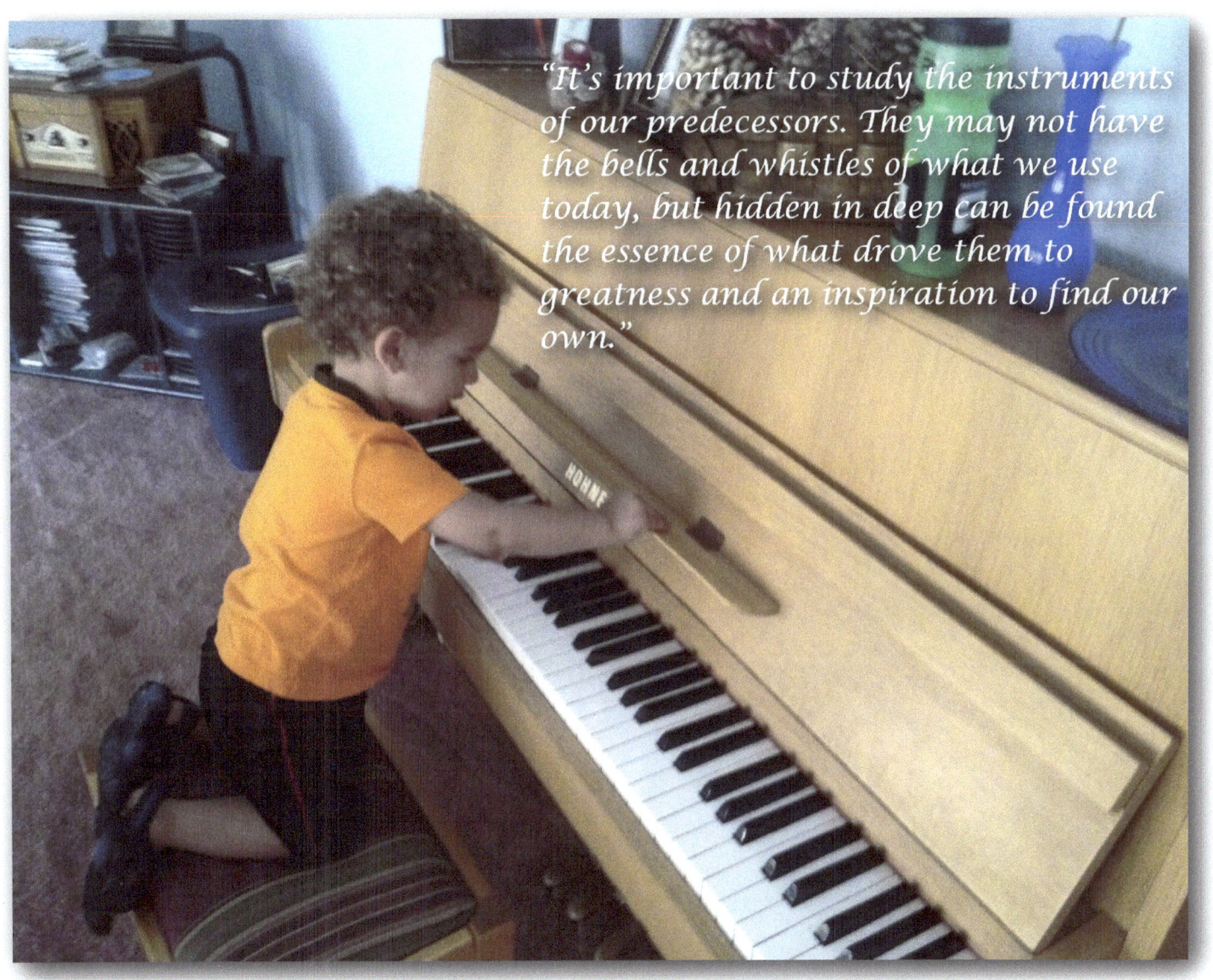

"It's important to study the instruments of our predecessors. They may not have the bells and whistles of what we use today, but hidden in deep can be found the essence of what drove them to greatness and an inspiration to find our own."

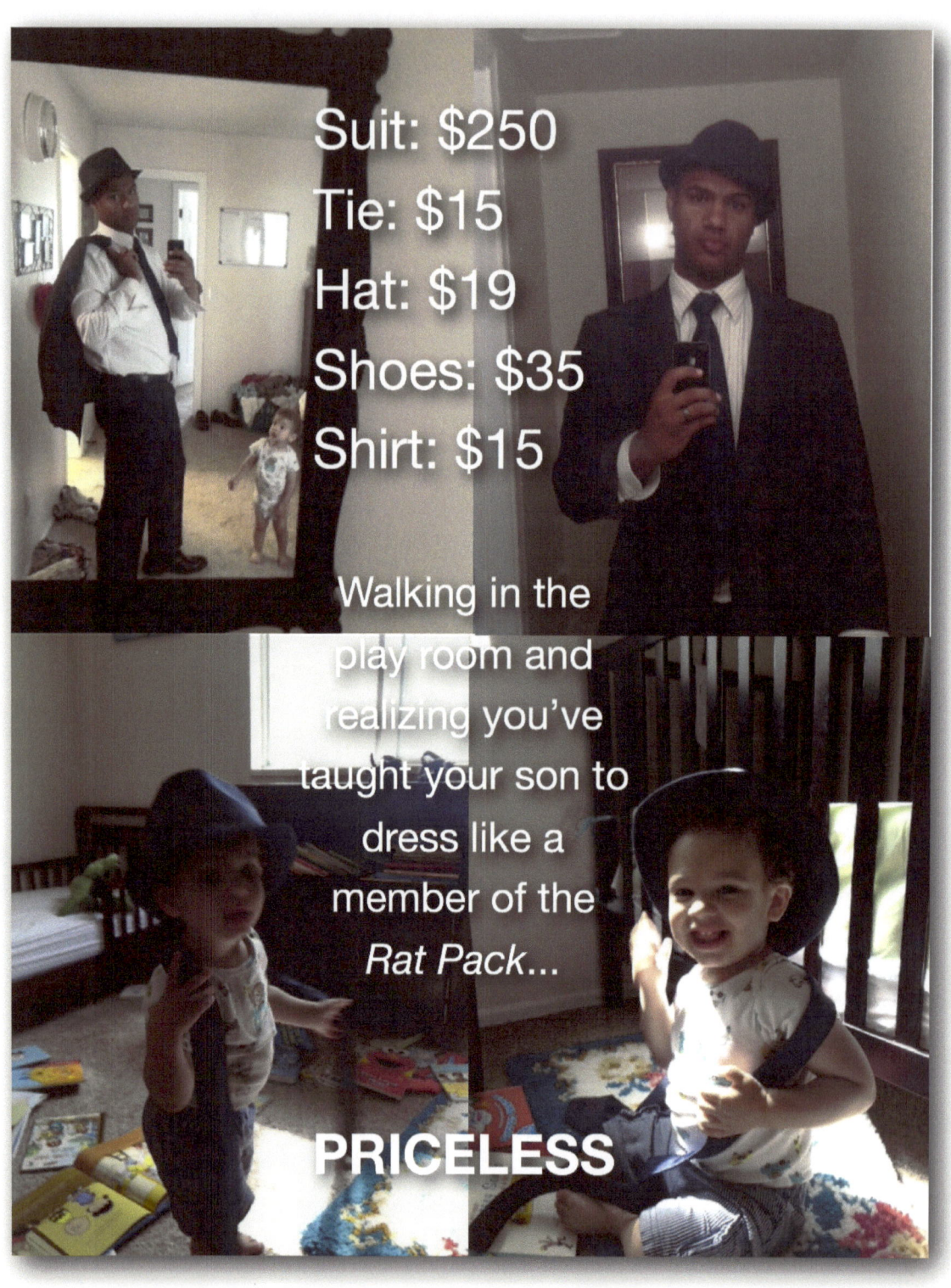

Suit: $250

Tie: $15

Hat: $19

Shoes: $35

Shirt: $15

Walking in the play room and realizing you've taught your son to dress like a member of the *Rat Pack*...

PRICELESS

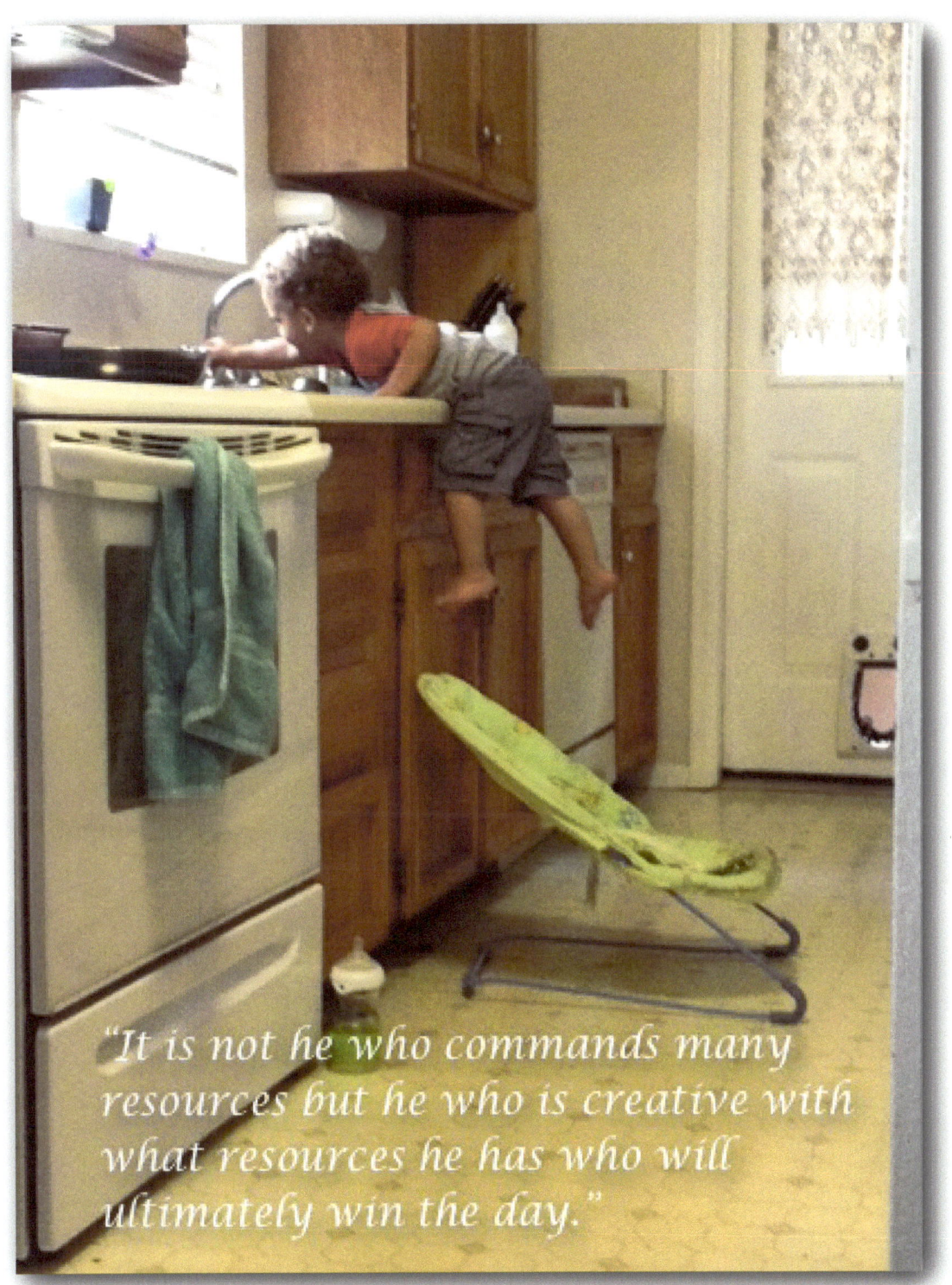

"It is not he who commands many resources but he who is creative with what resources he has who will ultimately win the day."

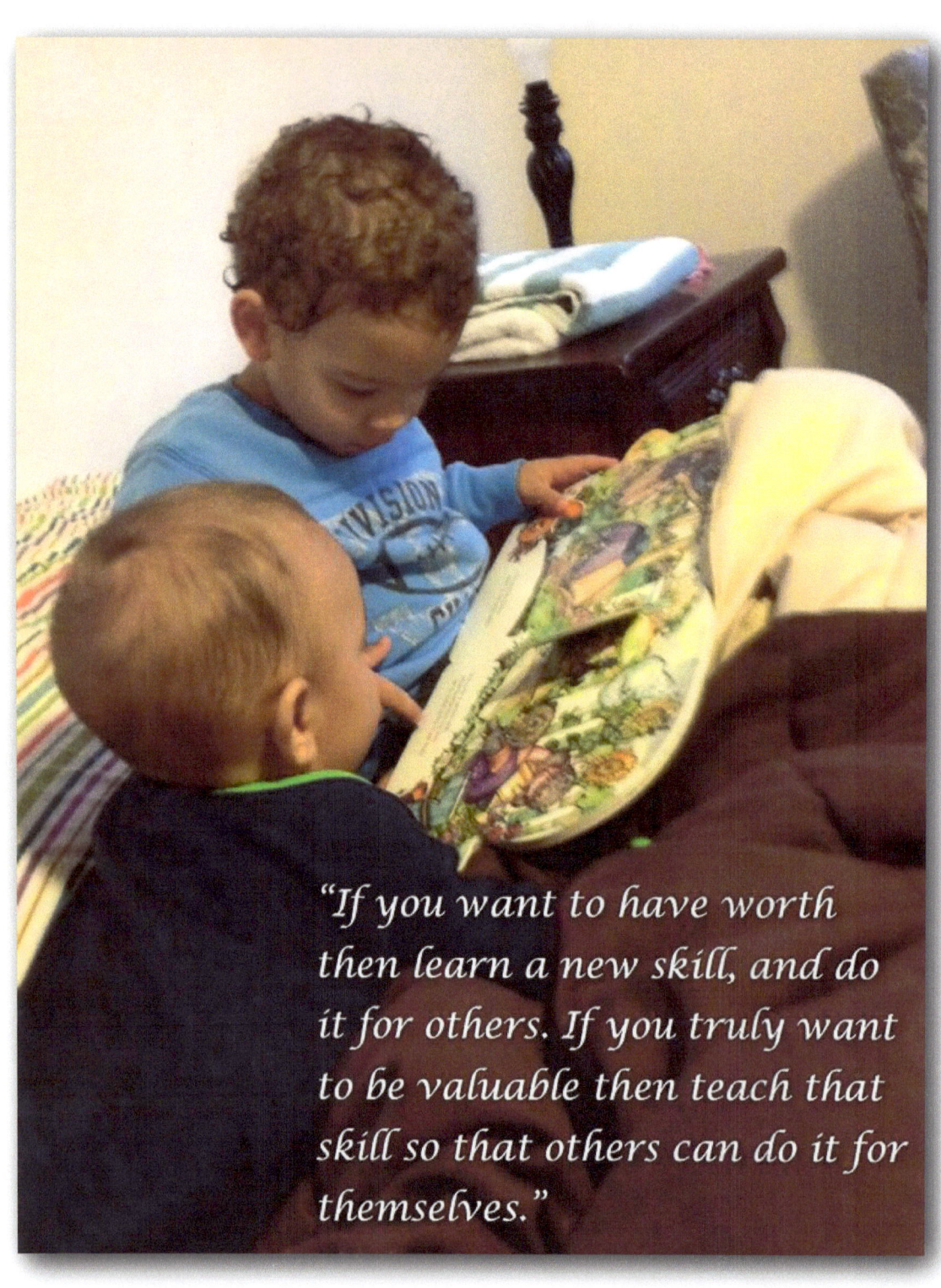

"If you want to have worth then learn a new skill, and do it for others. If you truly want to be valuable then teach that skill so that others can do it for themselves."

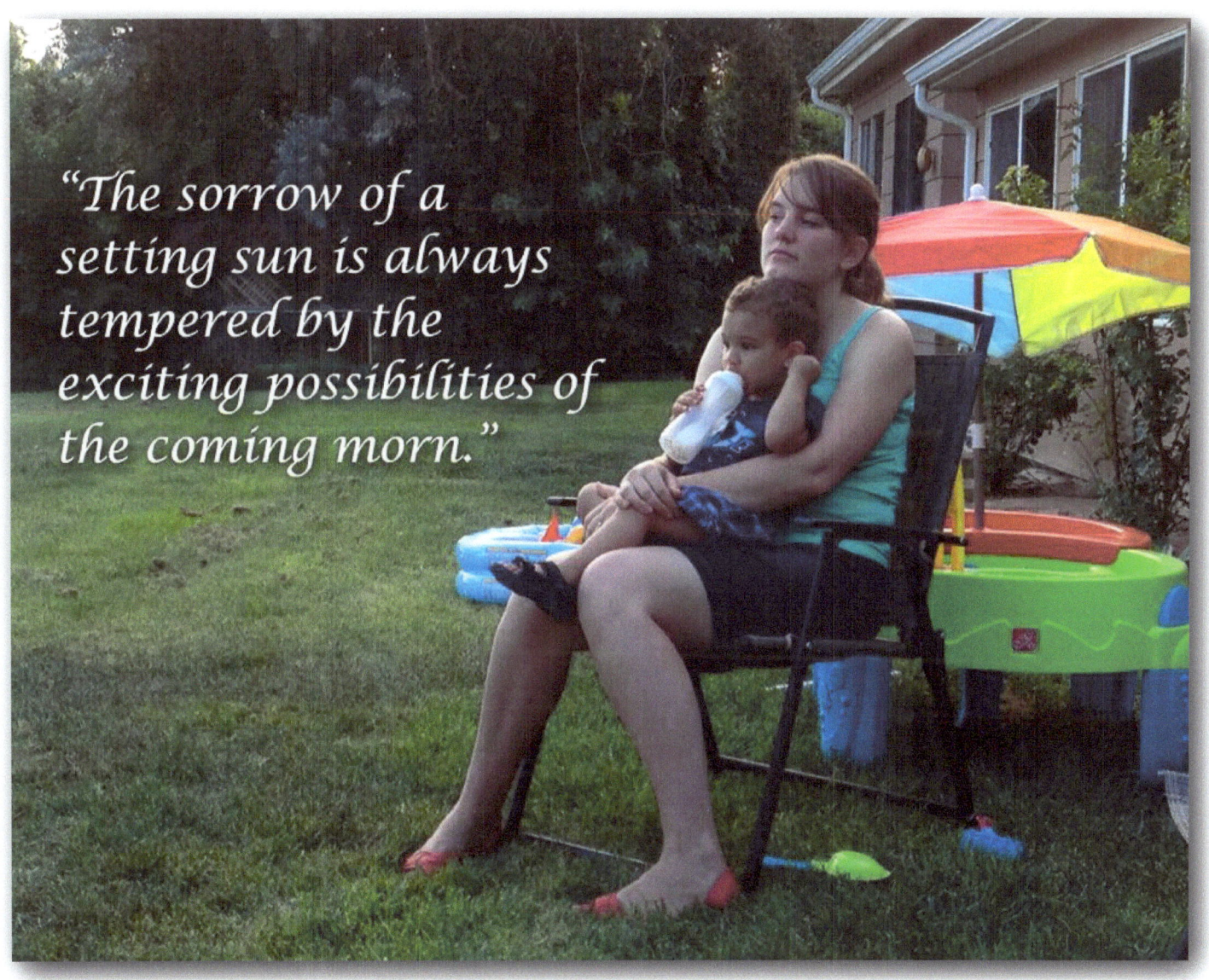

"The sorrow of a setting sun is always tempered by the exciting possibilities of the coming morn."

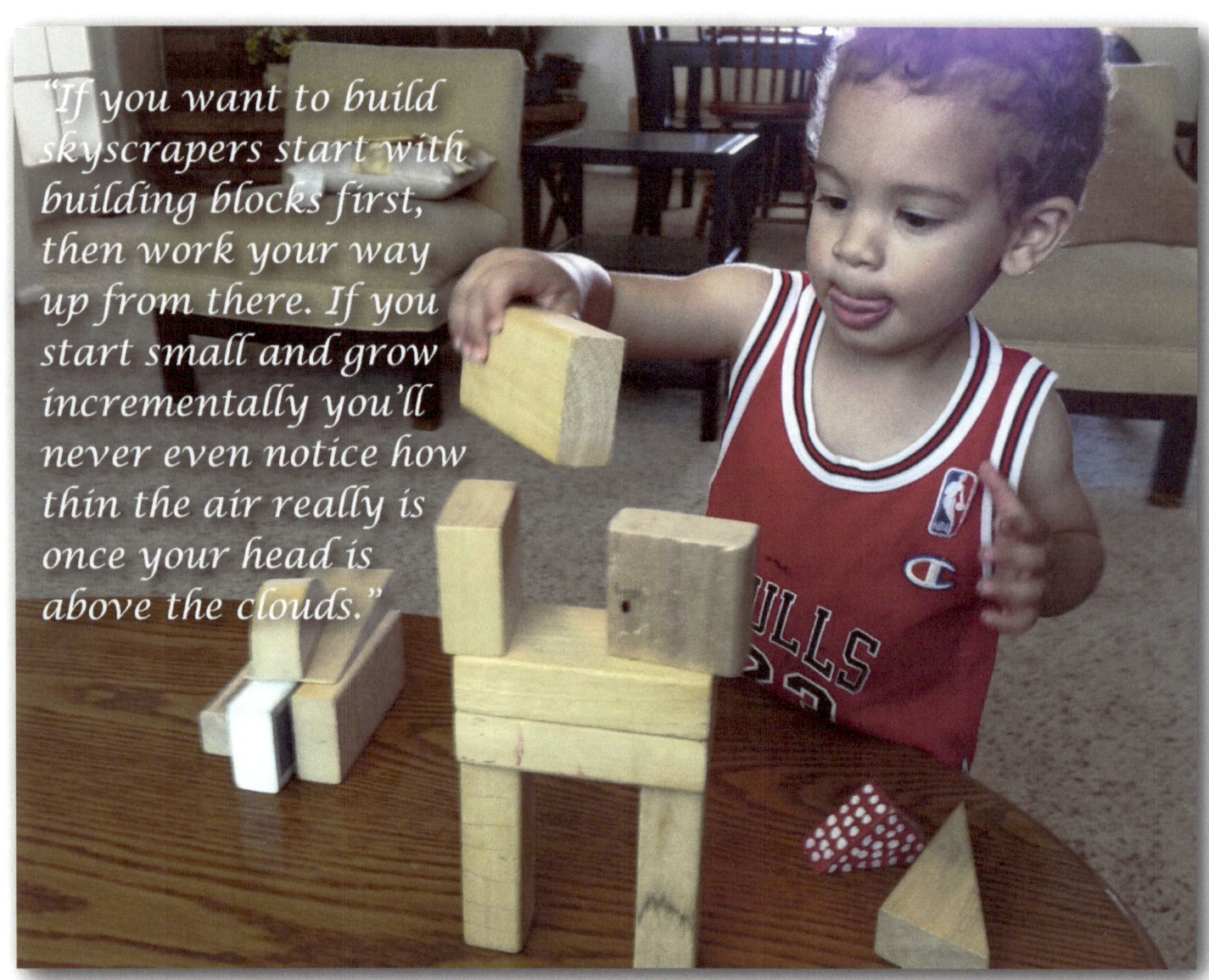

"If you want to build skyscrapers start with building blocks first, then work your way up from there. If you start small and grow incrementally you'll never even notice how thin the air really is once your head is above the clouds."

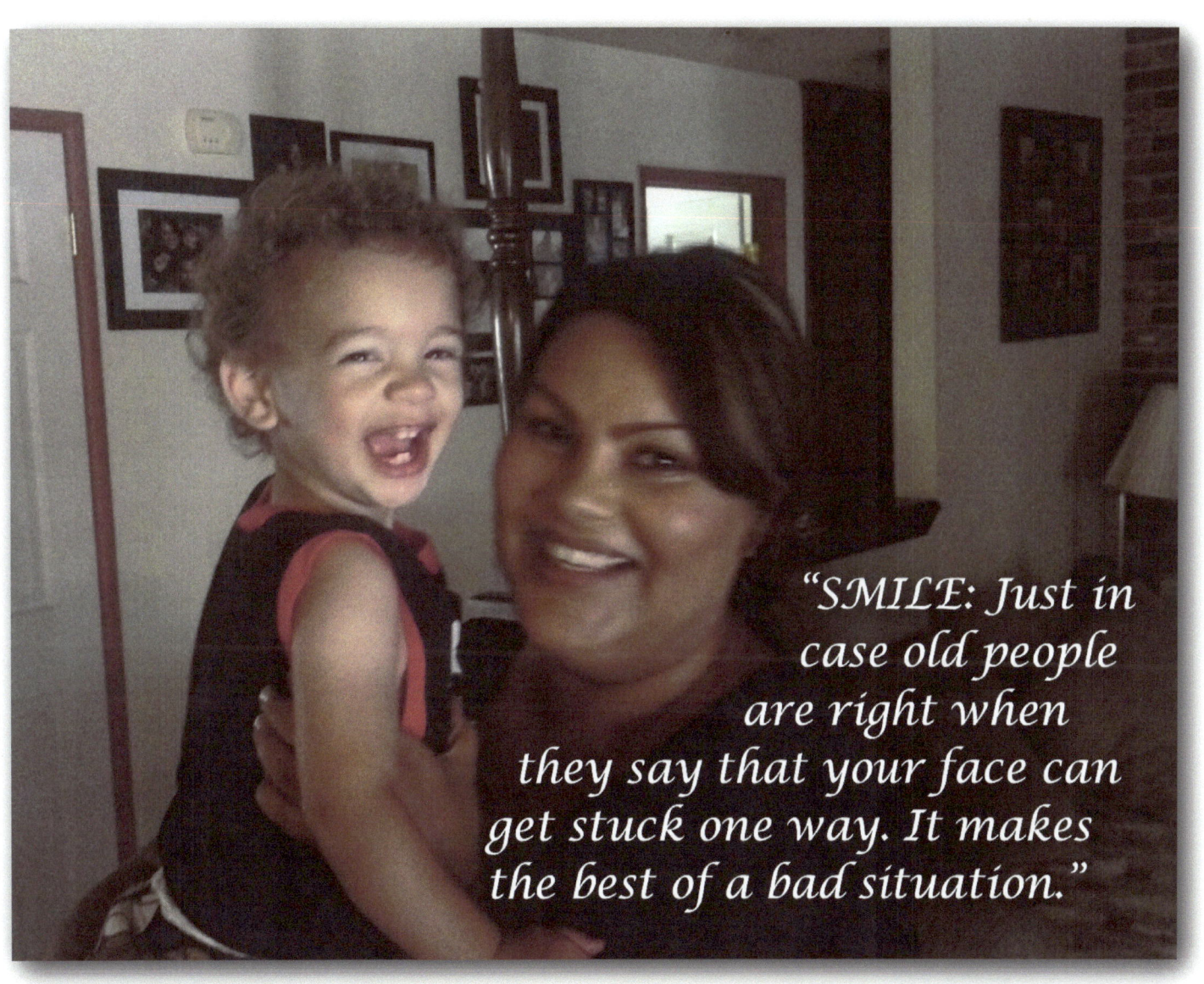

"SMILE: Just in case old people are right when they say that your face can get stuck one way. It makes the best of a bad situation."

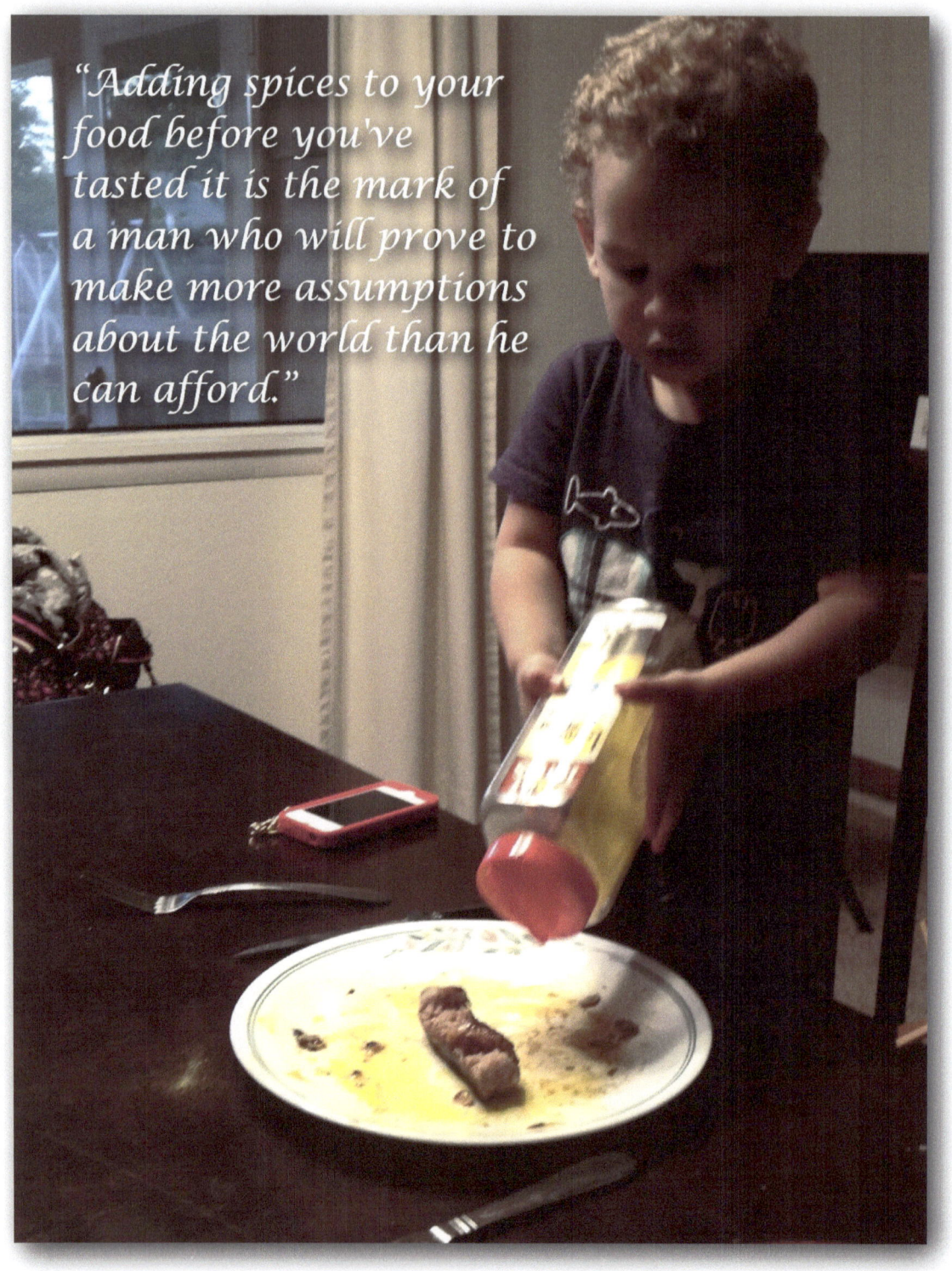

"*Adding spices to your food before you've tasted it is the mark of a man who will prove to make more assumptions about the world than he can afford.*"

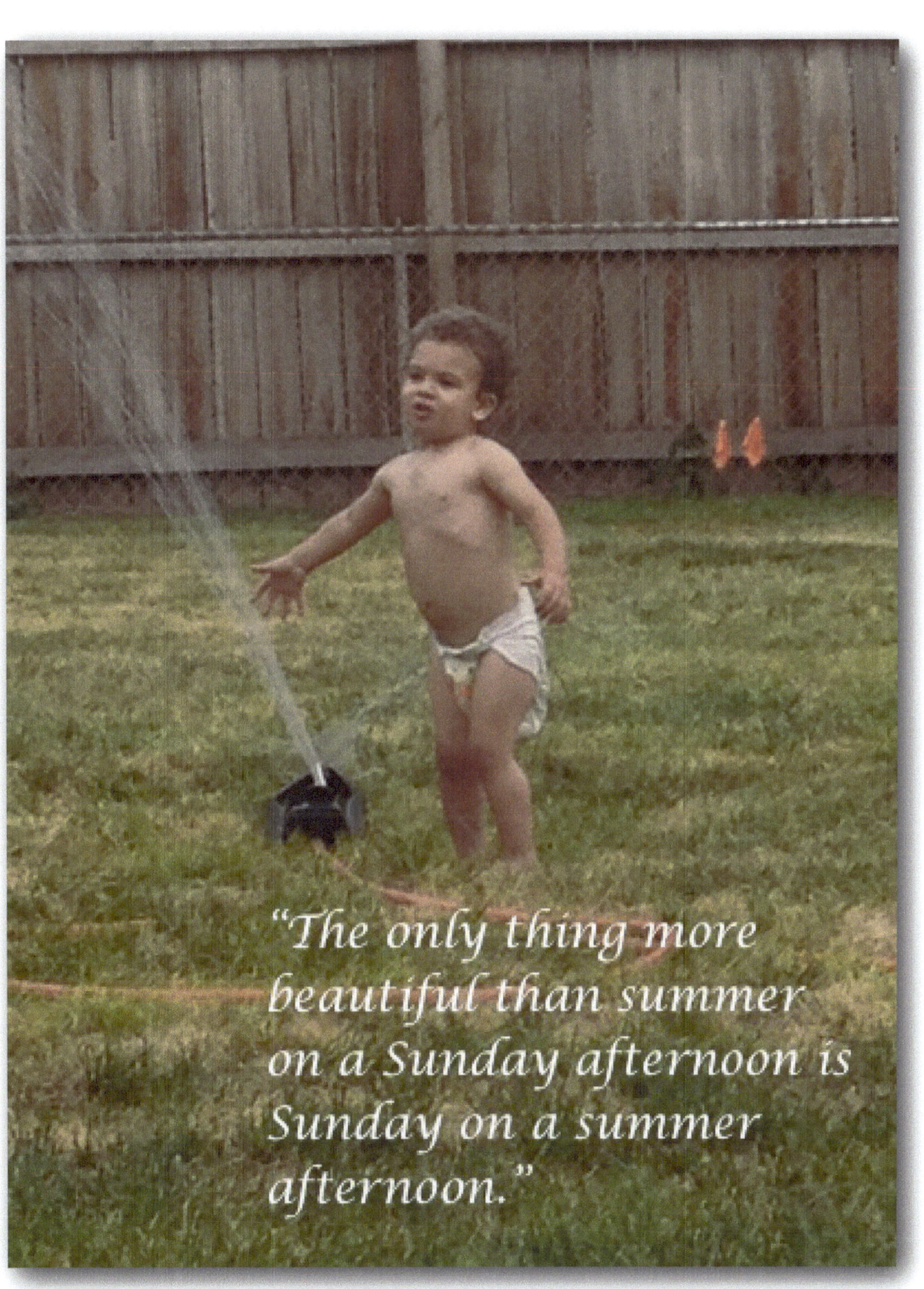

"The only thing more beautiful than summer on a Sunday afternoon is Sunday on a summer afternoon."

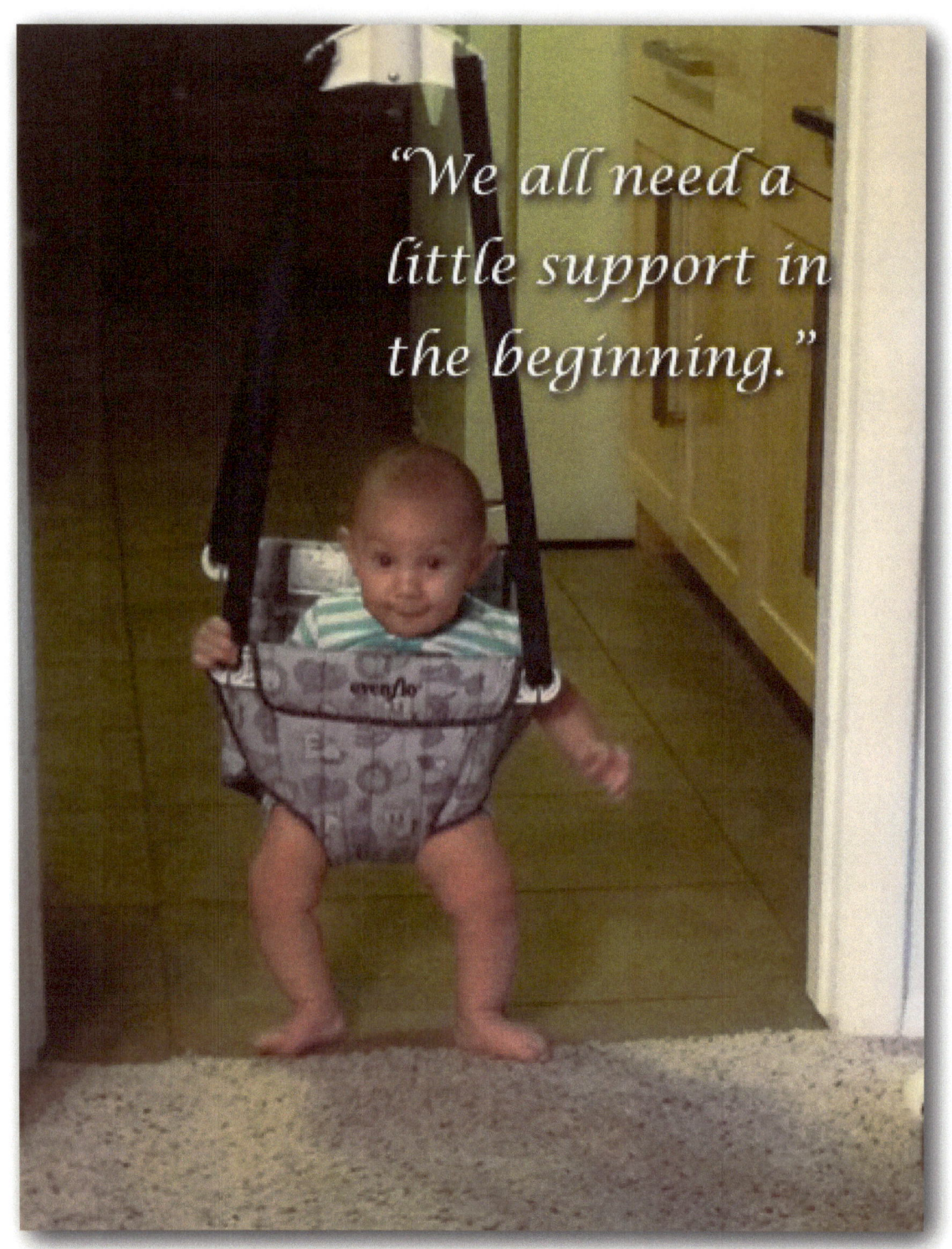

"We all need a little support in the beginning."

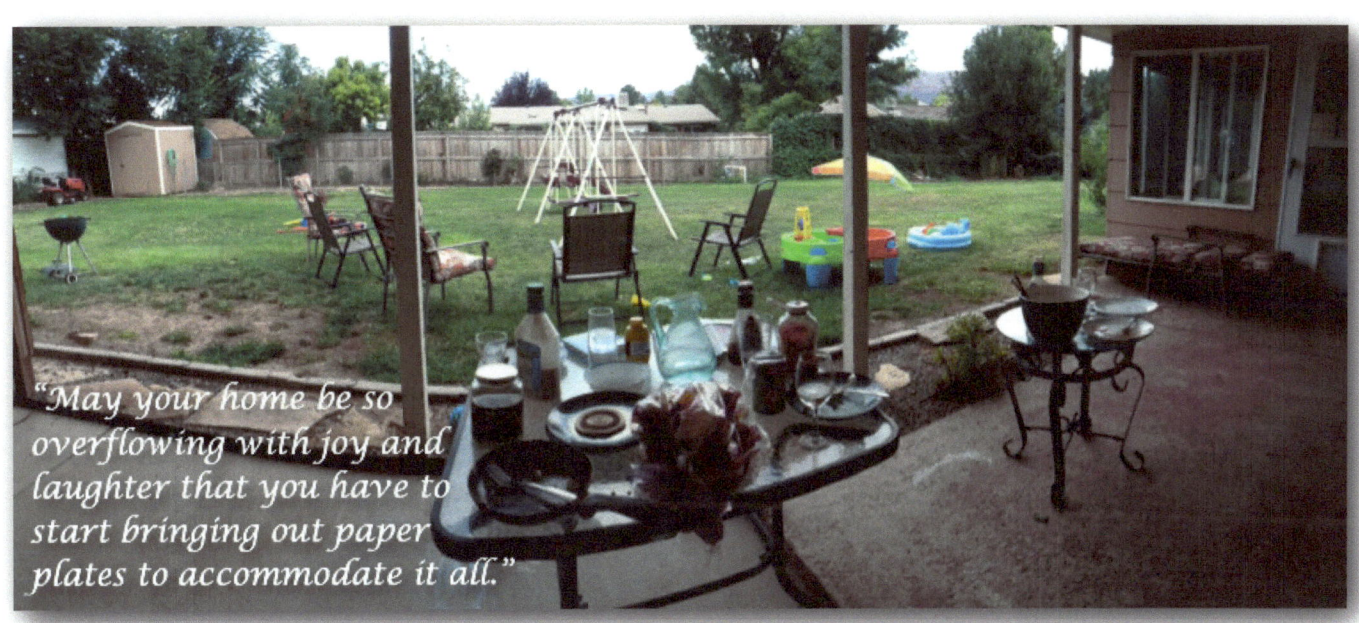

"May your home be so overflowing with joy and laughter that you have to start bringing out paper plates to accommodate it all."

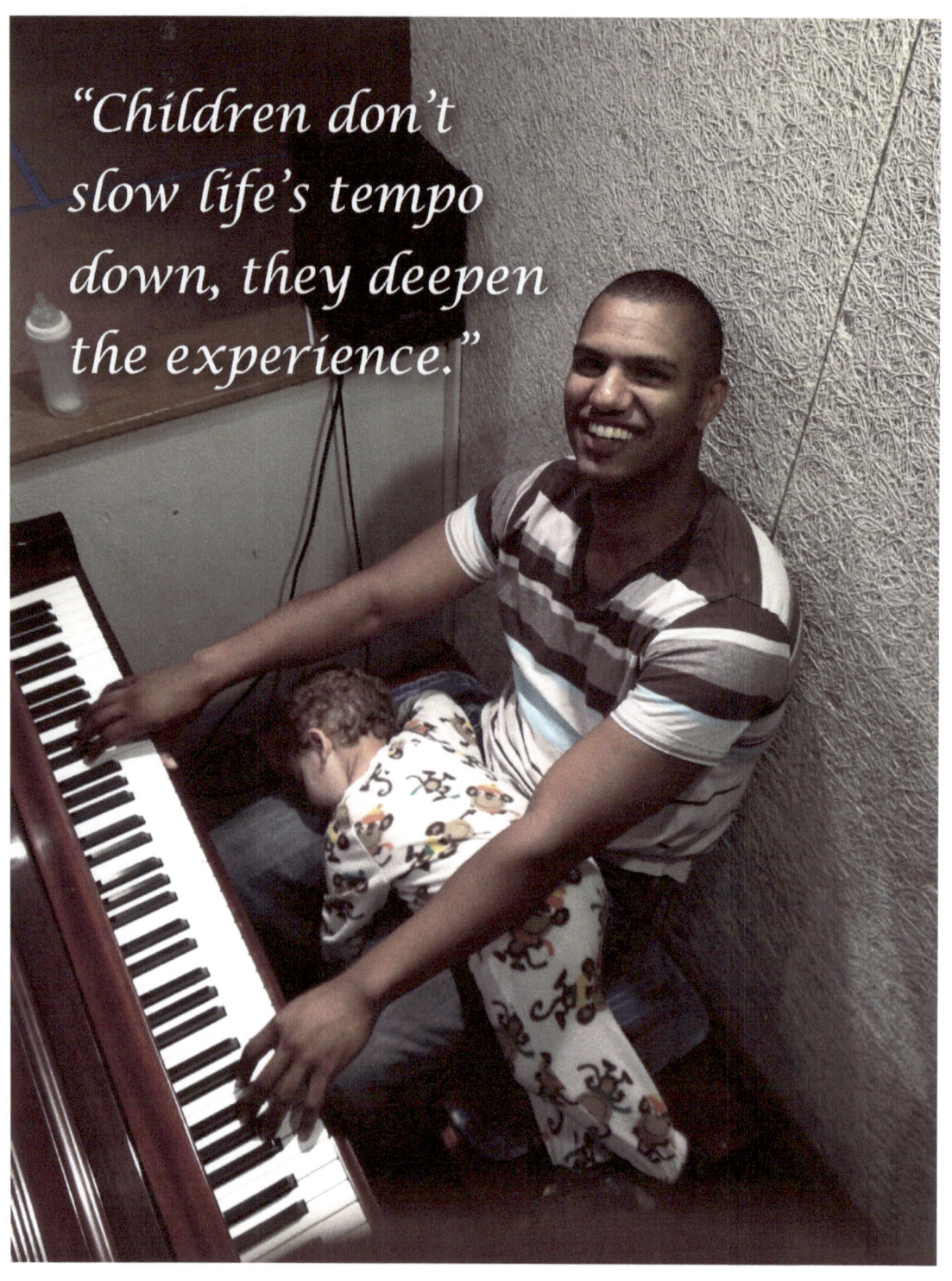

"Children don't slow life's tempo down, they deepen the experience."

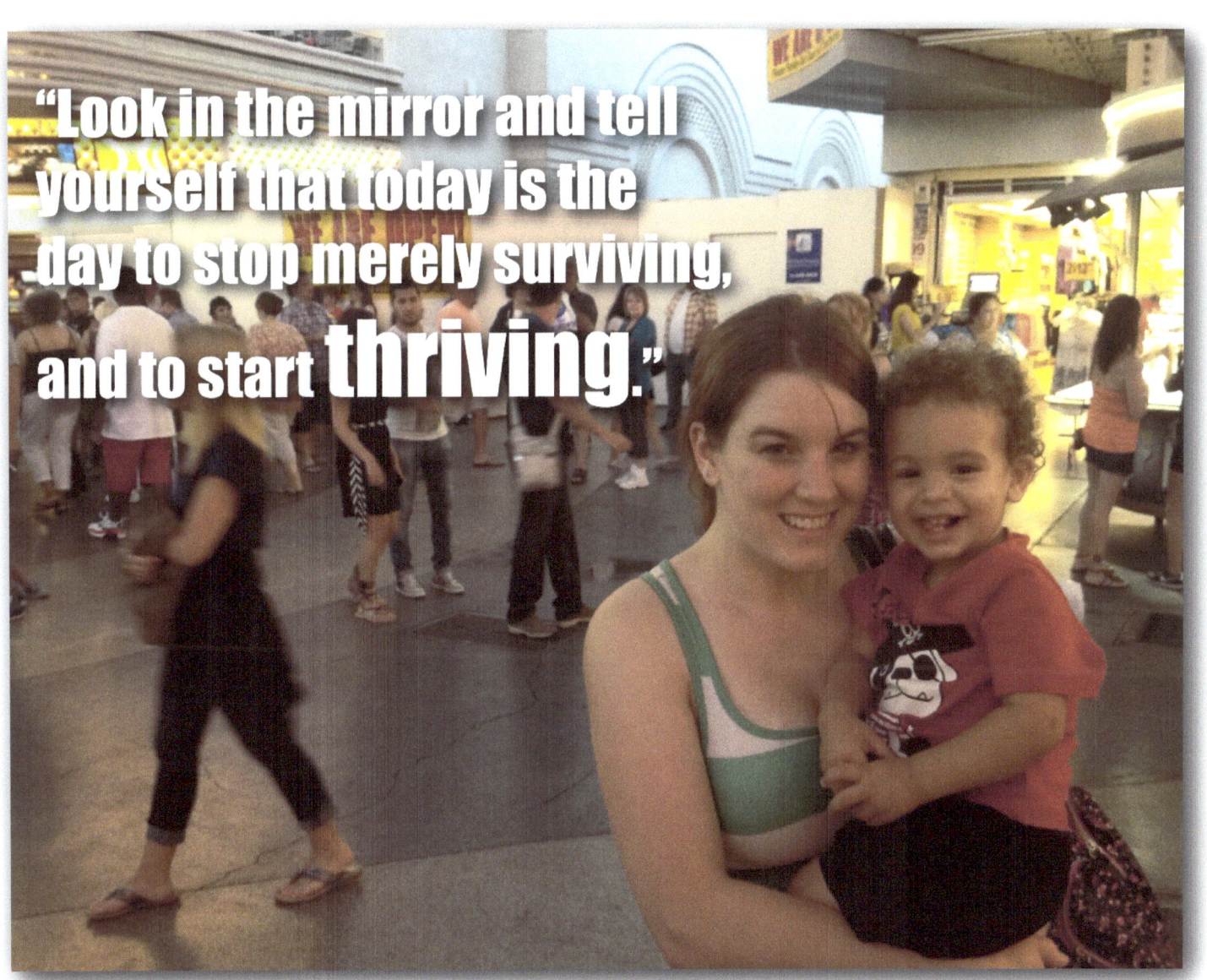

"Look in the mirror and tell yourself that today is the day to stop merely surviving, and to start **thriving**."

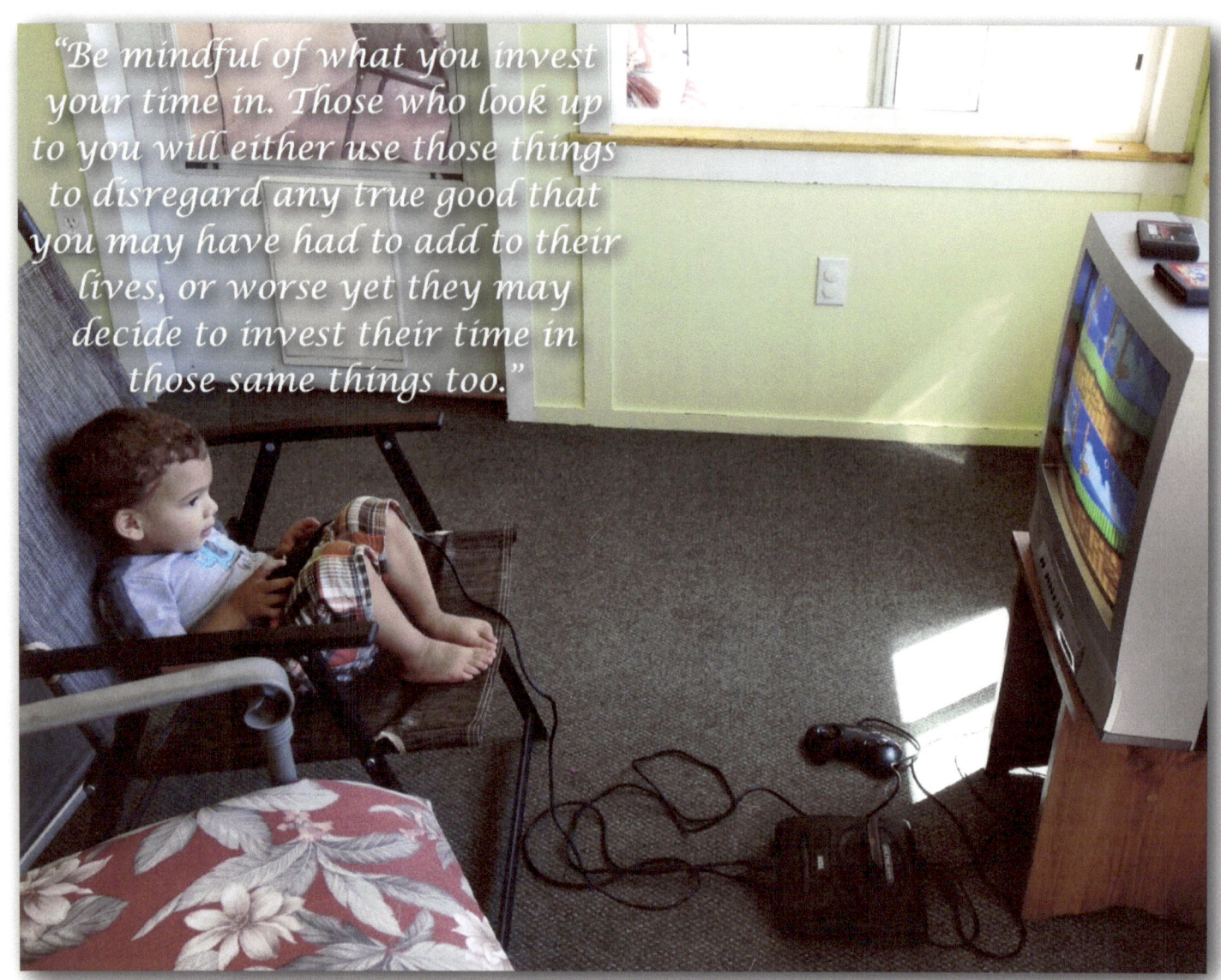

"Be mindful of what you invest your time in. Those who look up to you will either use those things to disregard any true good that you may have had to add to their lives, or worse yet they may decide to invest their time in those same things too."

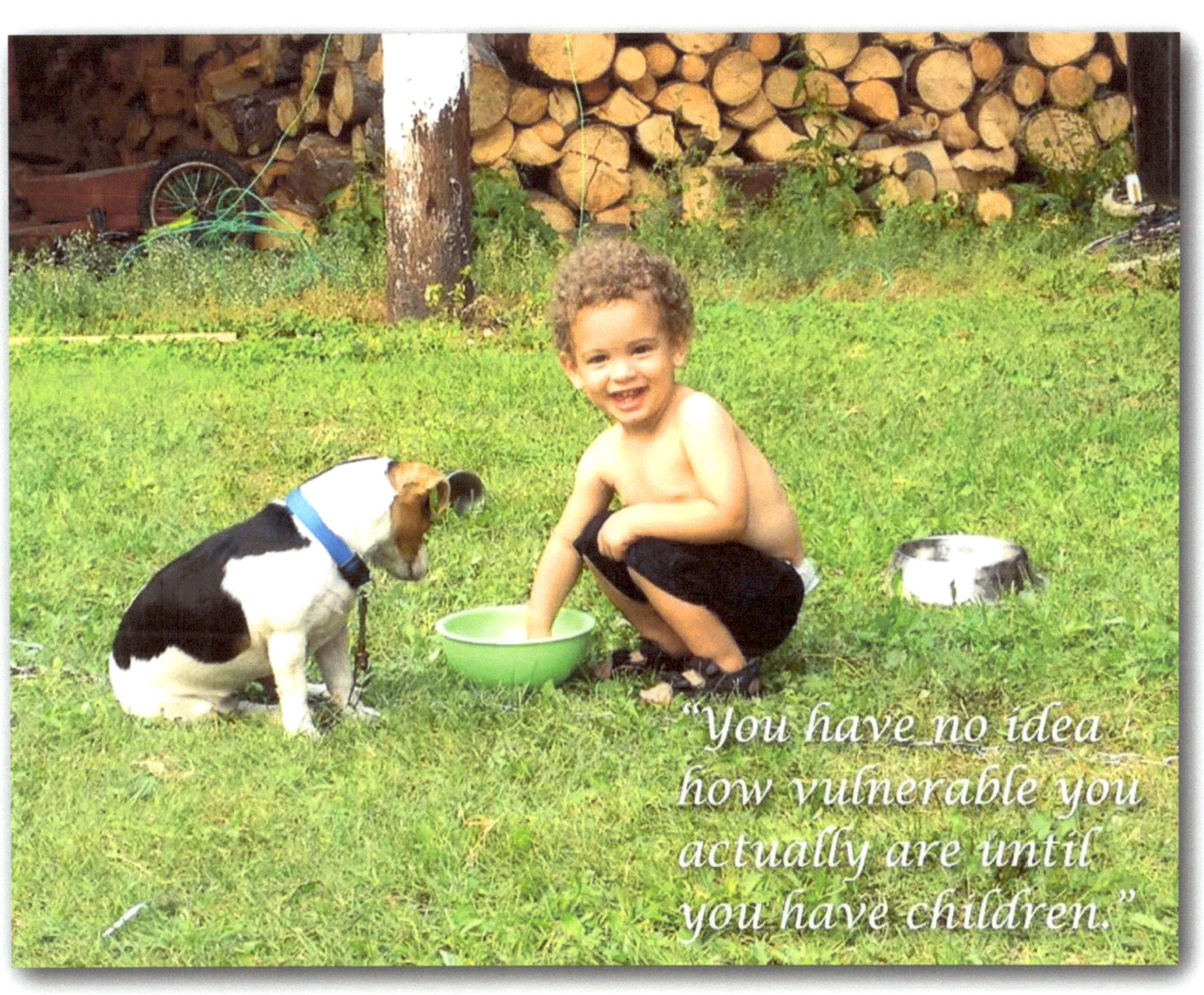

"You have no idea how vulnerable you actually are until you have children."

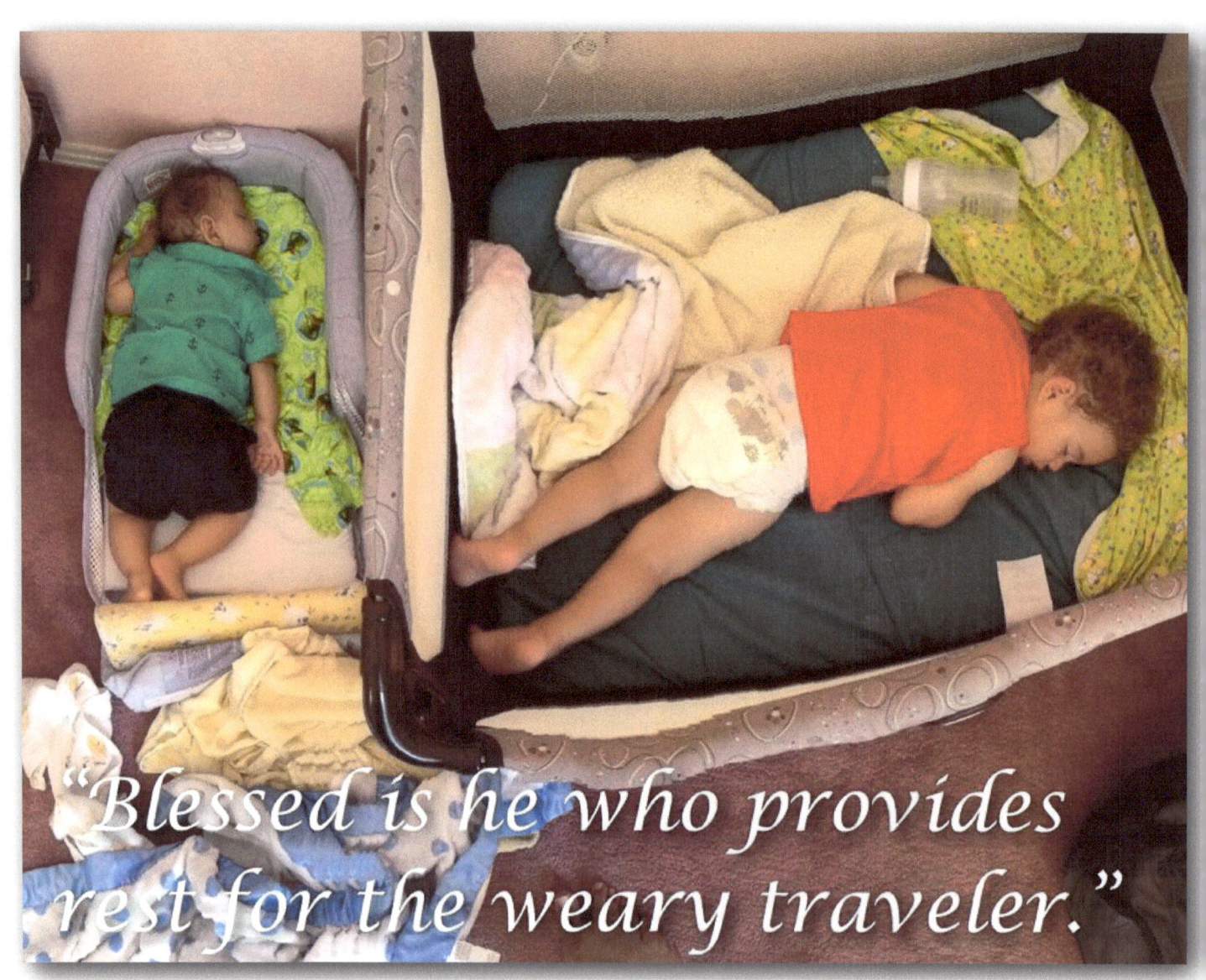

"Blessed is he who provides rest for the weary traveler."

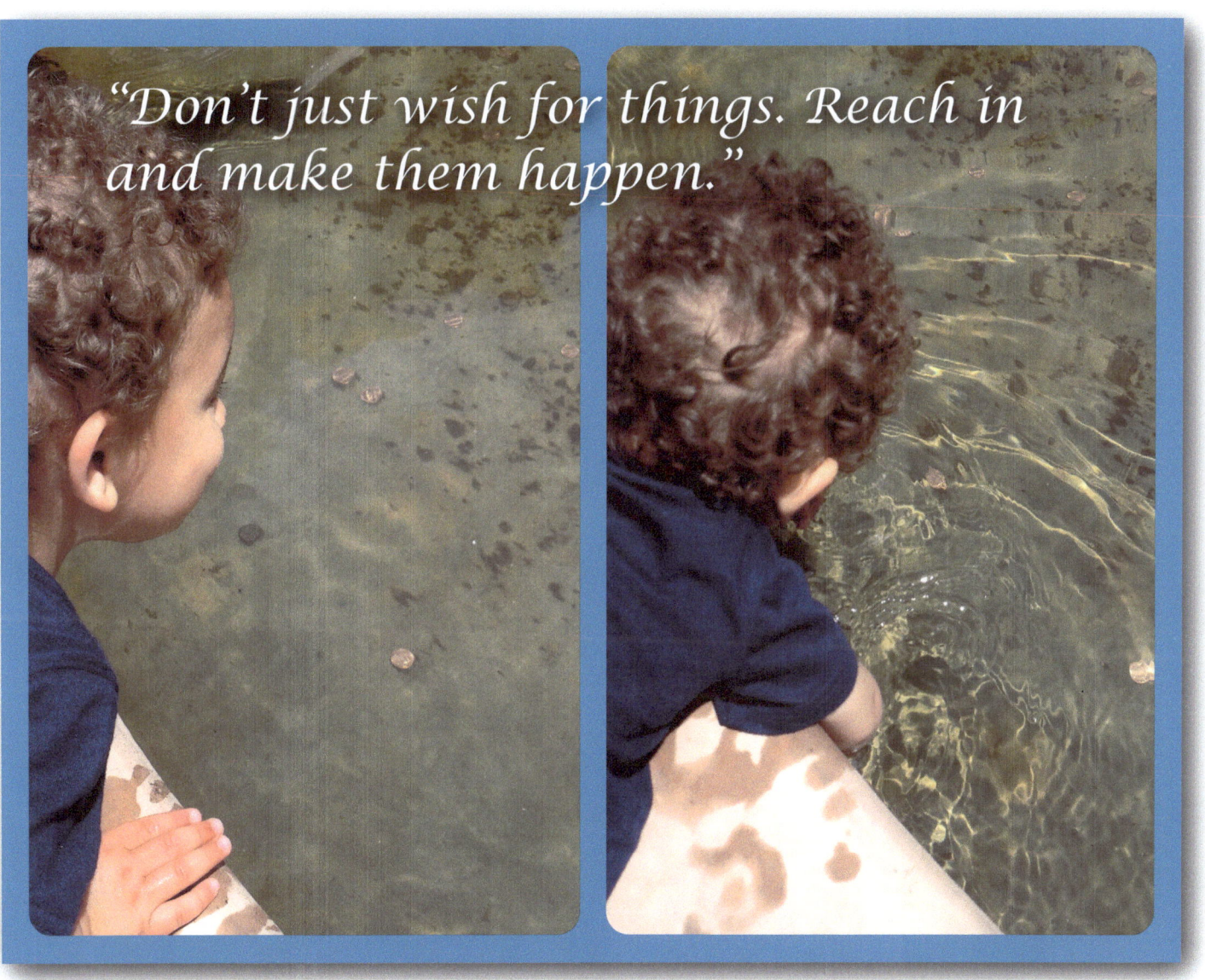

"Don't just wish for things. Reach in and make them happen."

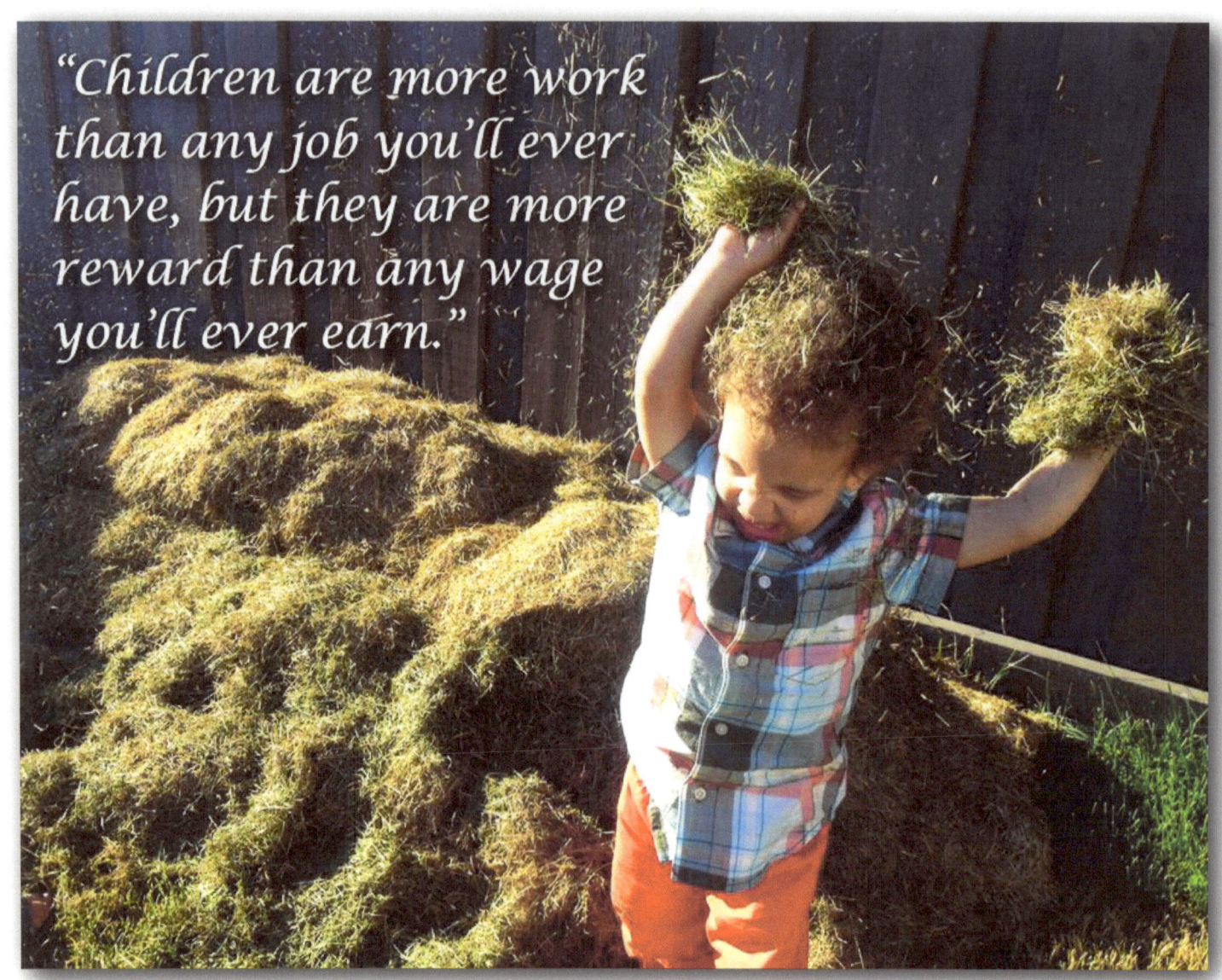

"Children are more work than any job you'll ever have, but they are more reward than any wage you'll ever earn."

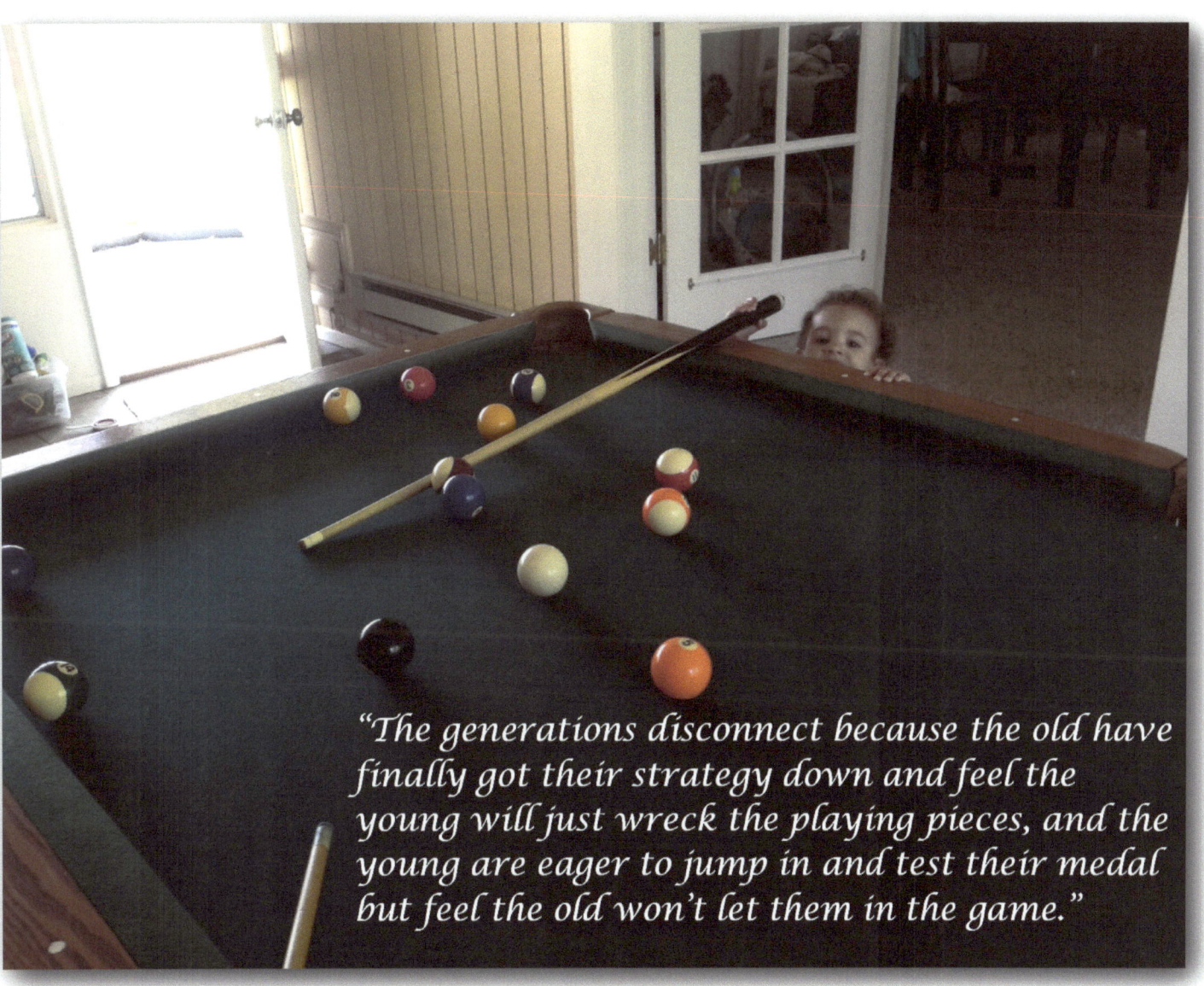

"The generations disconnect because the old have finally got their strategy down and feel the young will just wreck the playing pieces, and the young are eager to jump in and test their medal but feel the old won't let them in the game."

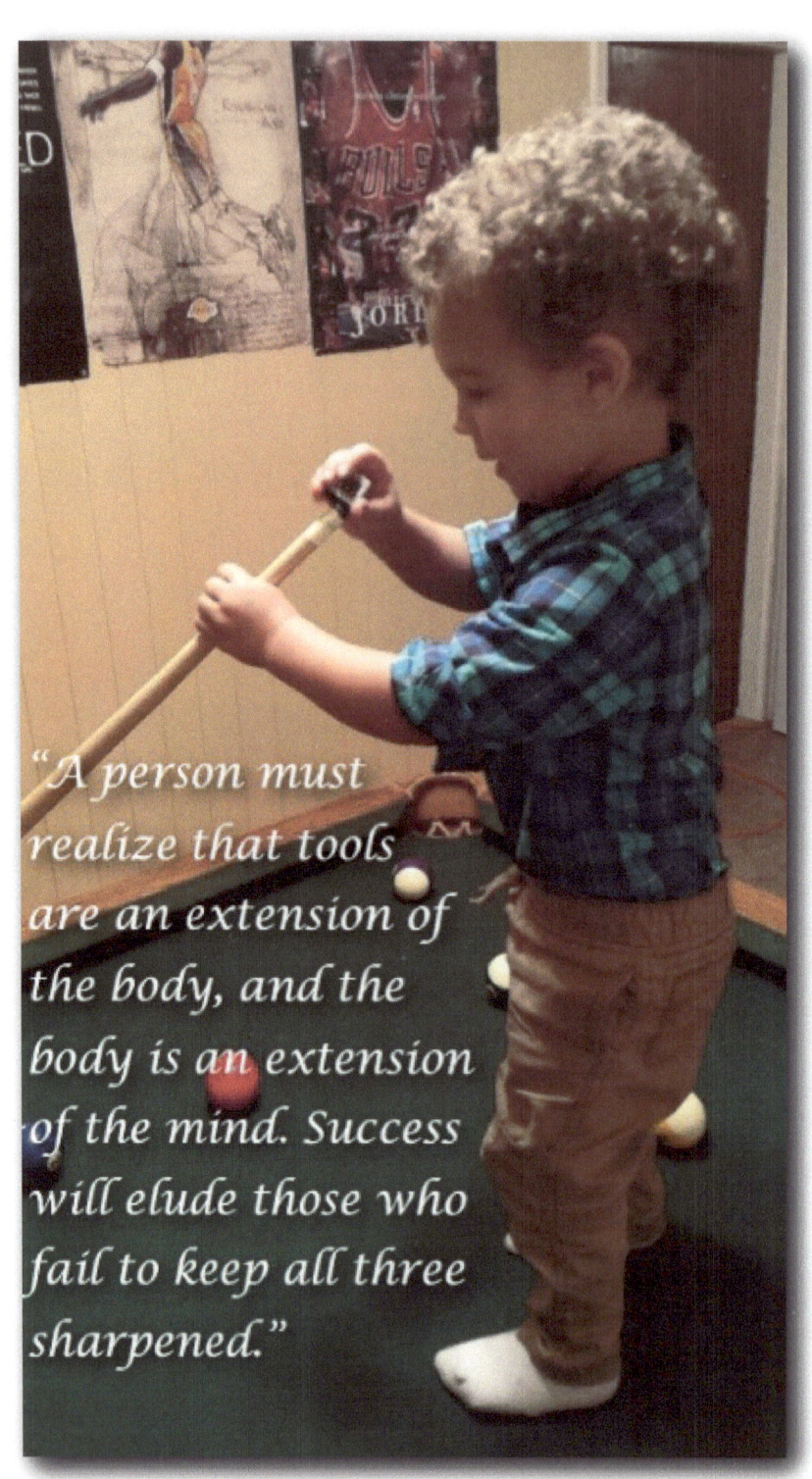

"A person must realize that tools are an extension of the body, and the body is an extension of the mind. Success will elude those who fail to keep all three sharpened."

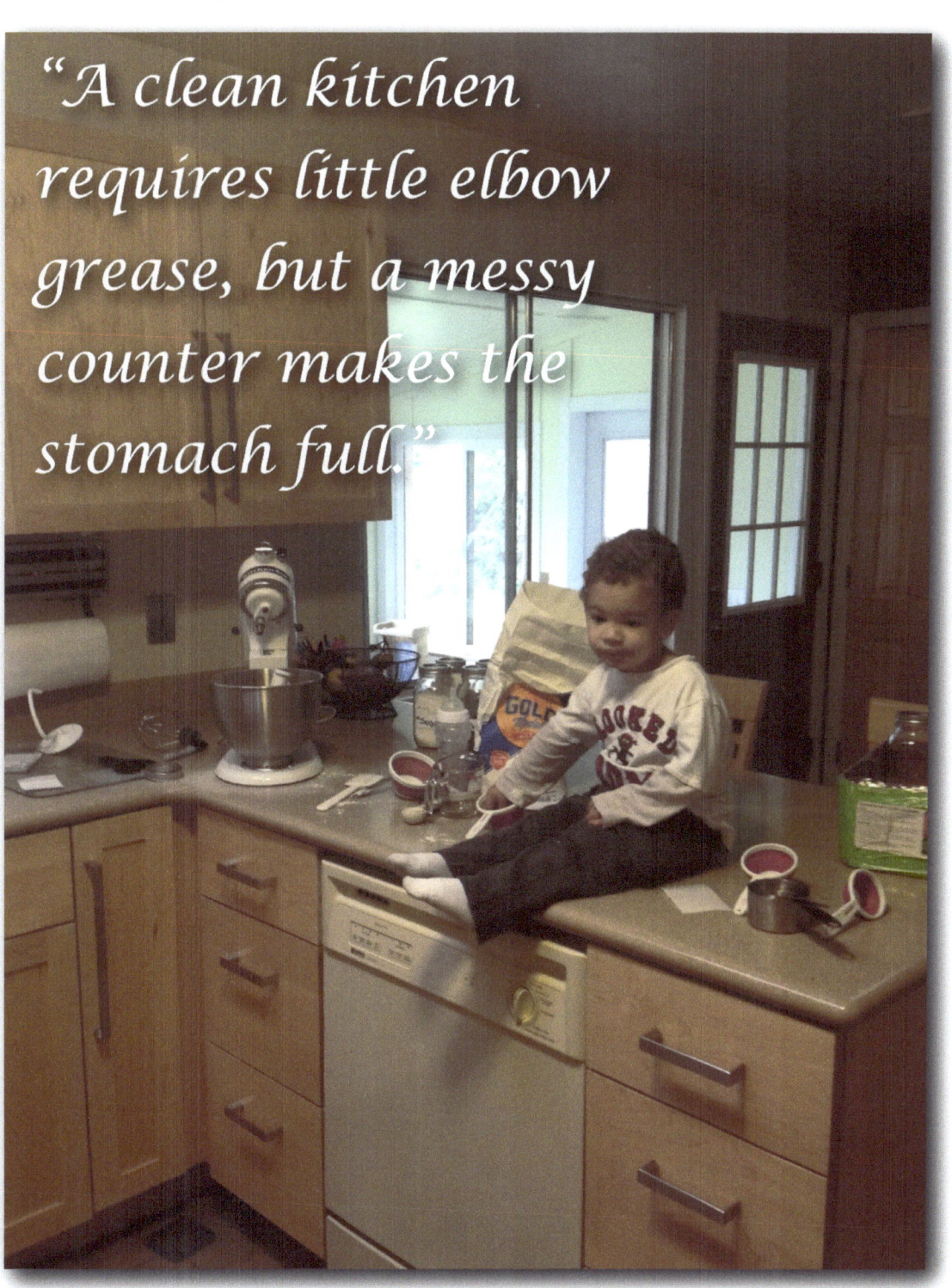

"A clean kitchen requires little elbow grease, but a messy counter makes the stomach full."

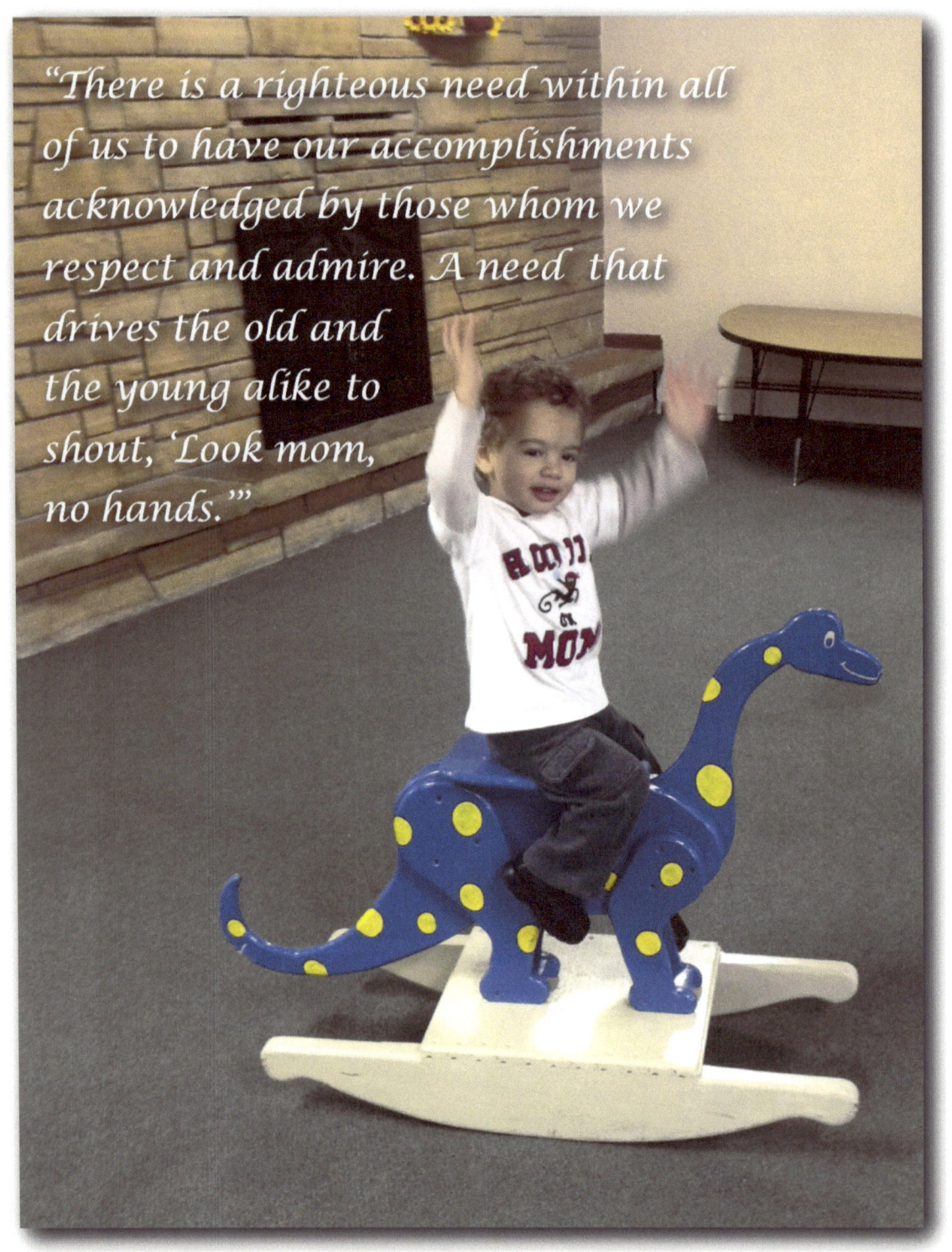

"There is a righteous need within all of us to have our accomplishments acknowledged by those whom we respect and admire. A need that drives the old and the young alike to shout, 'Look mom, no hands.'"

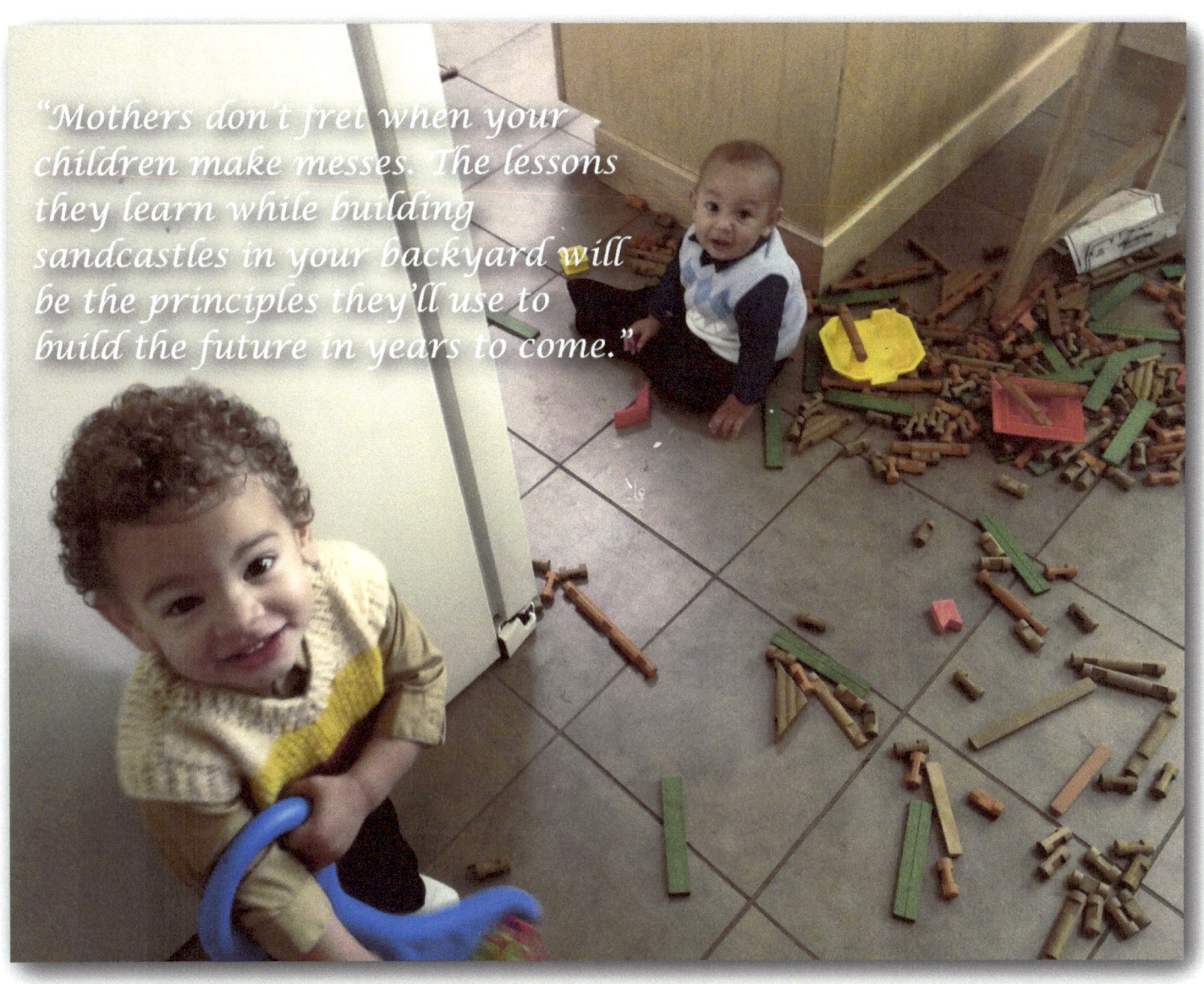

"Mothers don't fret when your children make messes. The lessons they learn while building sandcastles in your backyard will be the principles they'll use to build the future in years to come."

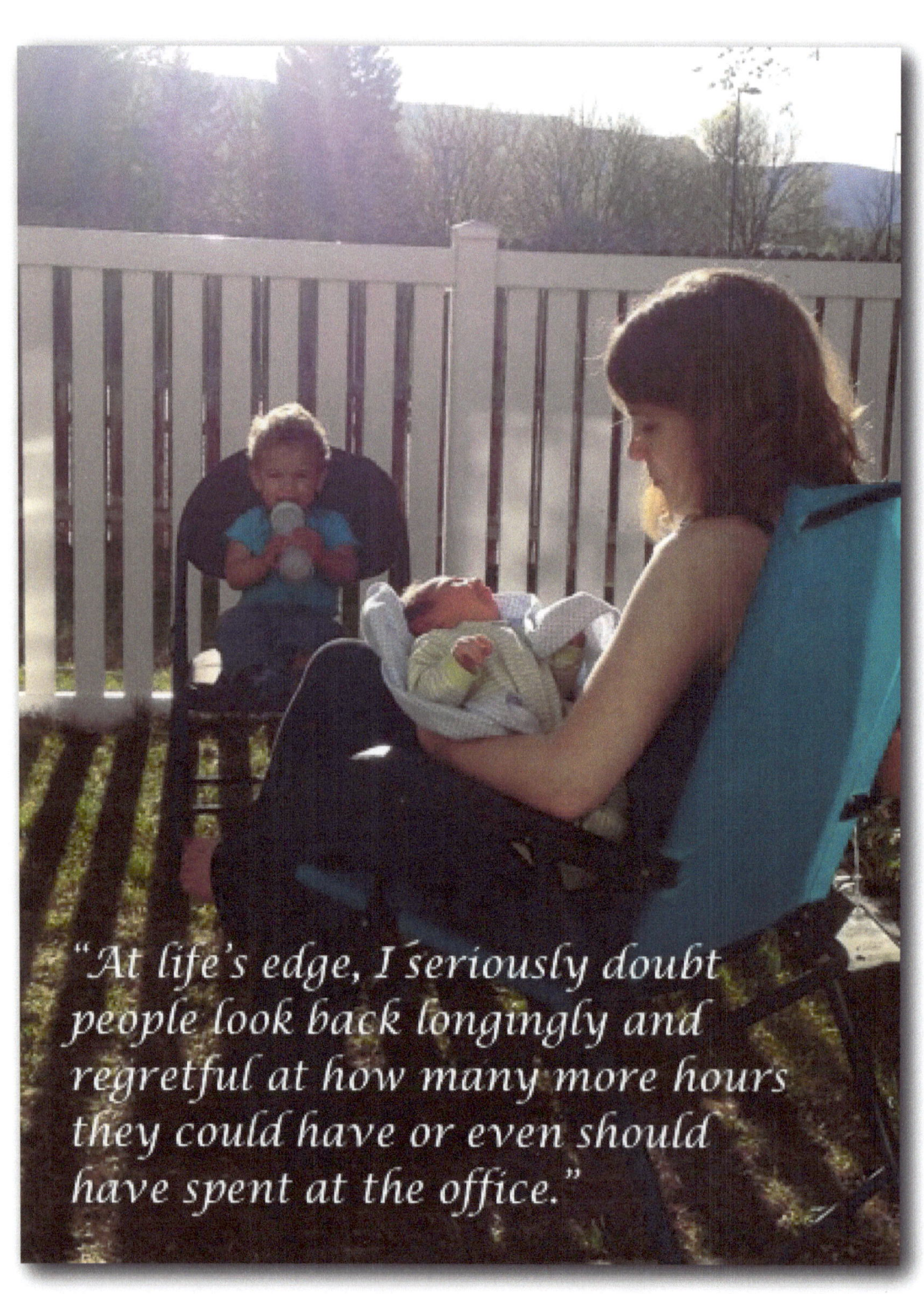

"At life's edge, I seriously doubt people look back longingly and regretful at how many more hours they could have or even should have spent at the office."

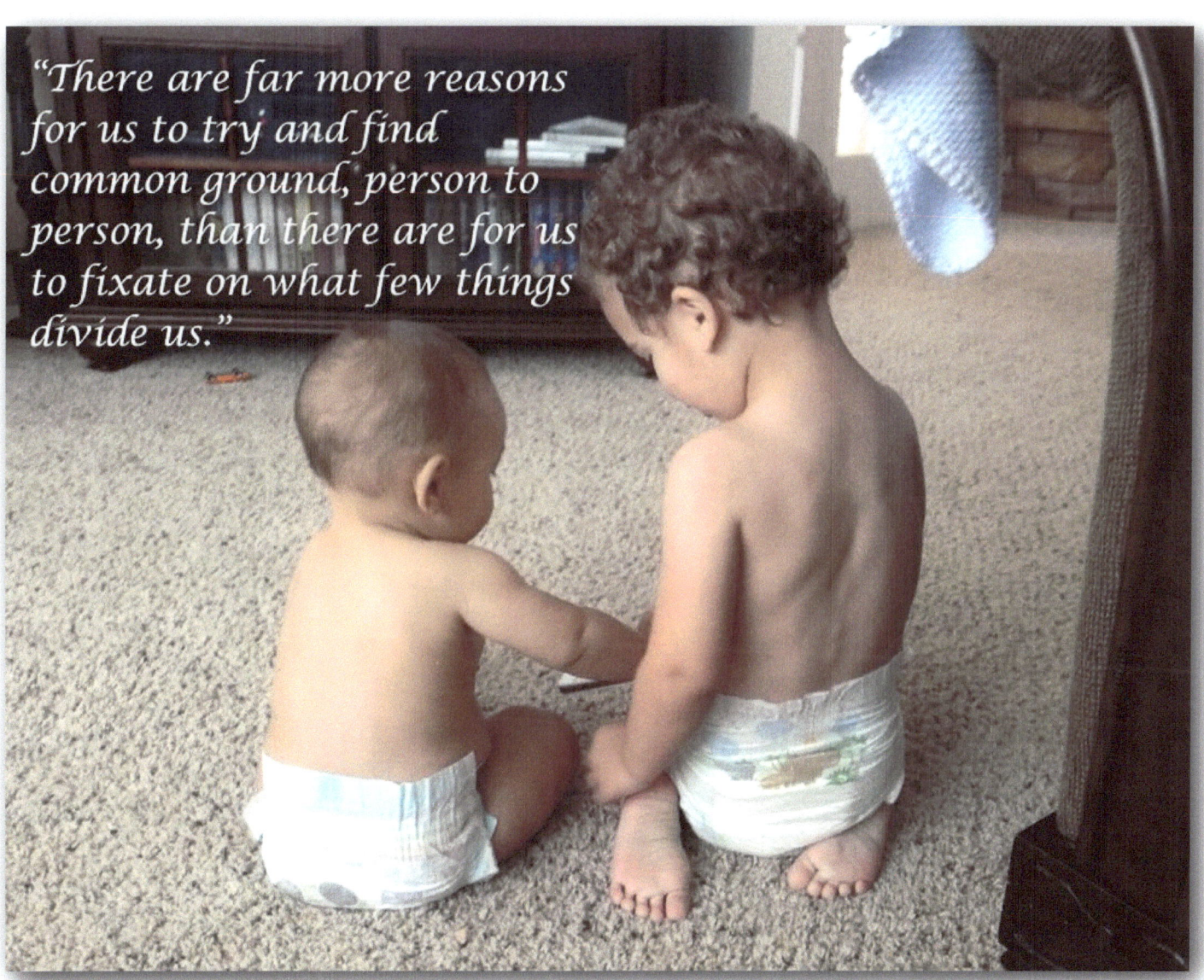

"There are far more reasons for us to try and find common ground, person to person, than there are for us to fixate on what few things divide us."

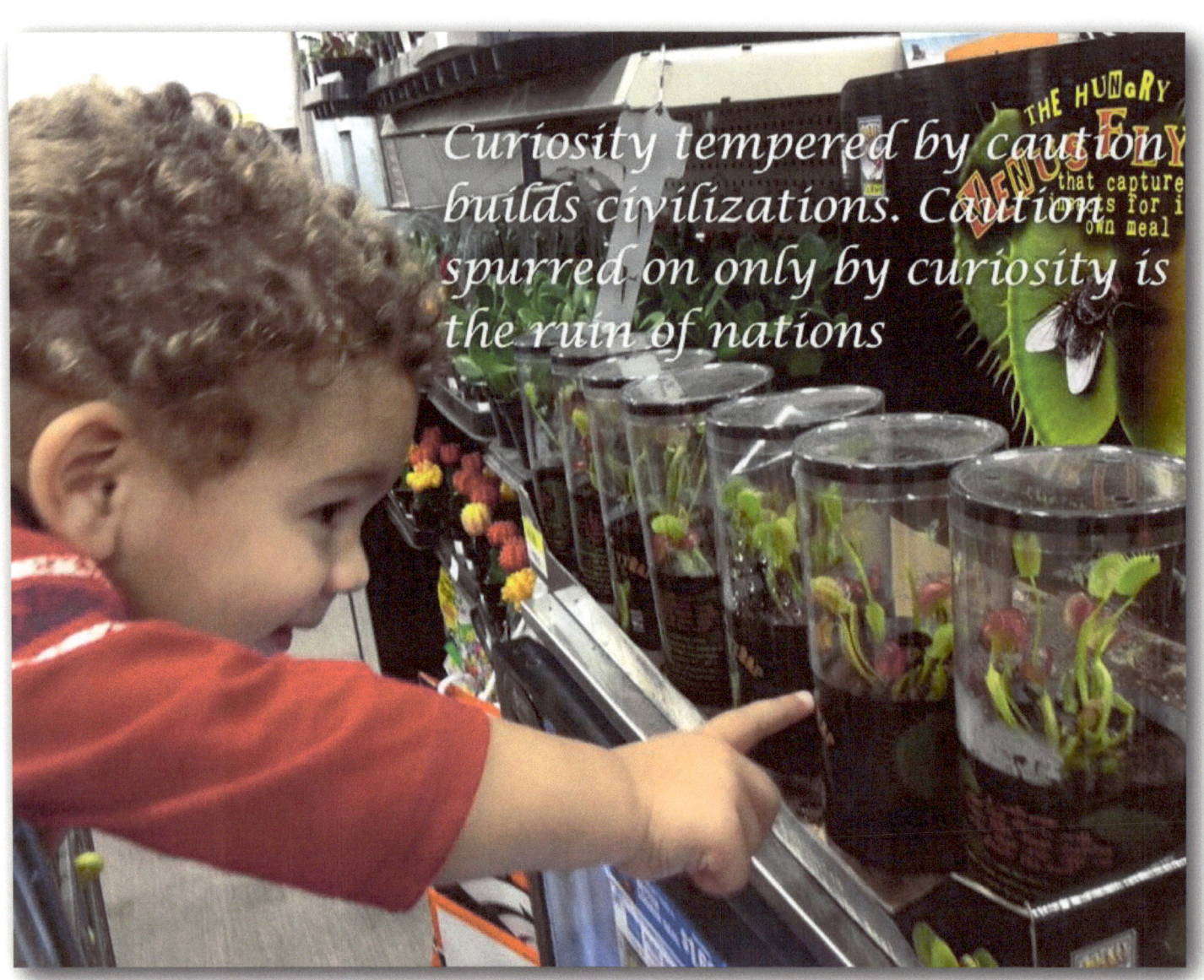

Curiosity tempered by caution builds civilizations. Caution spurred on only by curiosity is the ruin of nations

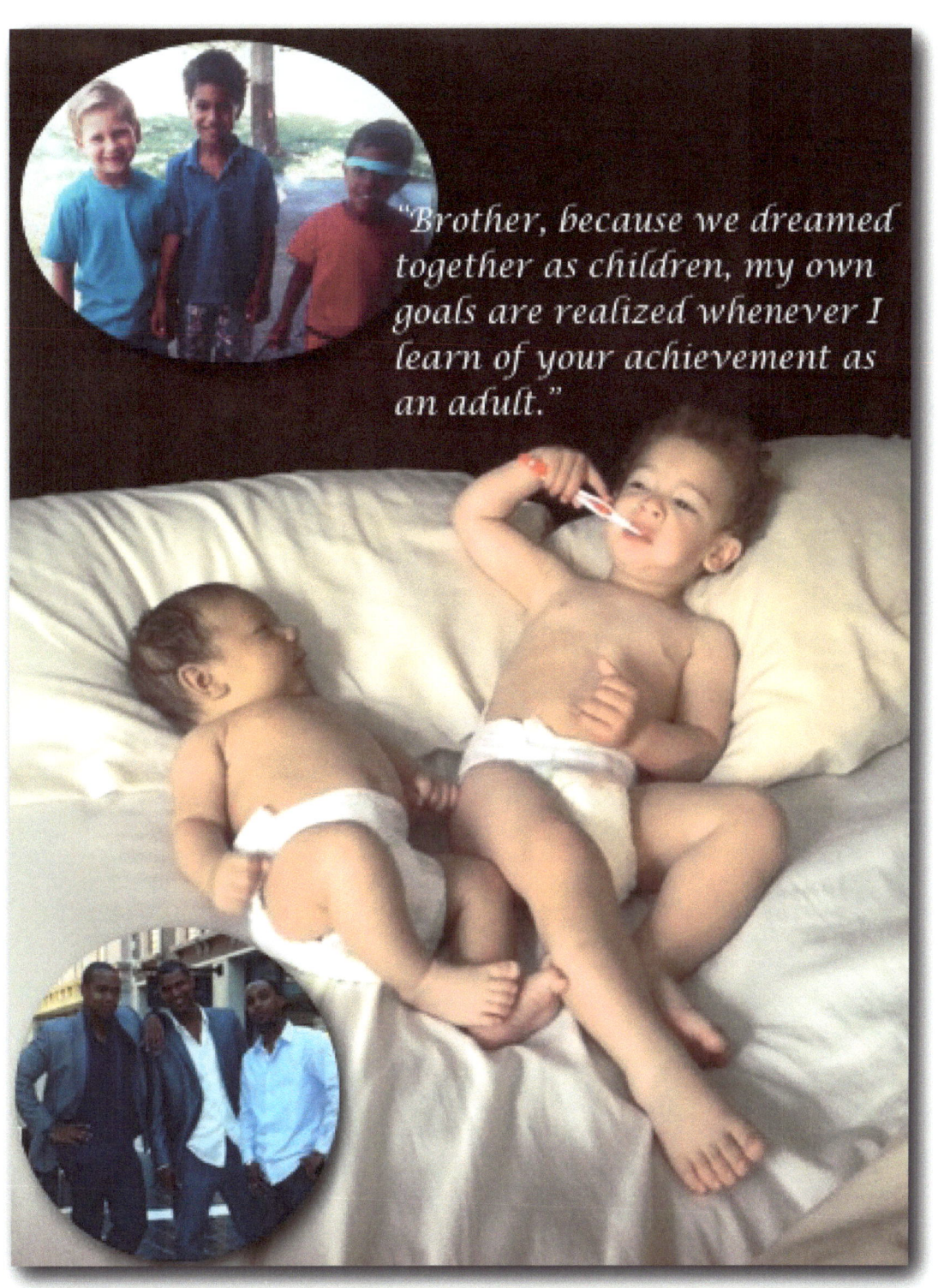

"Brother, because we dreamed together as children, my own goals are realized whenever I learn of your achievement as an adult."

For Quotes of the Day Merchandise please visit the online store at:

www.cafepress.com/degreesquotesoftheday

or follow the QR Code